OAK
Furniture
Styles and Prices

Revised and Expanded Edition

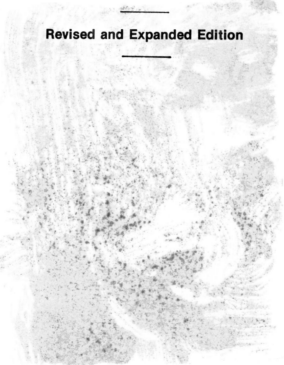

WH books

Published By

Wallace-Homestead Book Co.

Des Moines, Iowa

D1712009

ISBN: 0-87069-091-4

INTRODUCTION

Around the turn of the century, oak was one of the favorite woods for furniture. It was rare indeed for a home not to have at least one piece of good, sturdy oak . . . a desk (roll top, of course!) or bookcase or perhaps a china cabinet.

Because oak stands up well under years of use, furniture made from this solid wood abounds today. Overlooked for years by collectors and dealers, oak furniture now has come into its own and prices are rising.

The illustrations in this book were taken from an 1897 Montgomery Ward Furniture catalog. Montgomery Ward shipped furniture all over the United States and was particularly strong in the middle west where a great deal of this type furniture can still be found today. The same furniture was also available through other retail outlets besides Montgomery Ward.

Descriptions are the same as the original catalog and the prices in small letters were the 1897 prices. Today's average retail market price is indicated in larger type under each illustration.

The complete description of each item enables the dealer and collector to make an accurate identification of this furniture.

The prices in this book are average, retail prices for items in good, original condition. Restored items would be higher. All prices given are for pieces in oak. The same item in mahogany would usually run 20% higher, other woods about 10% higher than the oak price. Prices were arrived at after consultations with antique furniture dealers. Prices would be somewhat higher in the eastern part of the United States and in the far western states. Several dealers have estimated that prices will increase 30% or more over the next two years.

Oak furniture is still plentiful, however, and it presents many opportunities for collectors and dealers to accumulate good pieces at moderate prices.

Index of Categories

Published in United States of America by
WALLACE-HOMESTEAD BOOK COMPANY
Des Moines, Iowa 50305

Odd Pieces for the Parlor

No. 801 Fancy Chair. A handsome design for the hall or parlor. Mahogany veneered back and beautifully inlaid. Richly polished. Weight, 11 pounds. Mahogany finish only.
Price $4.50

$40-$50

No. 2750. This beautiful odd chair is upholstered in all colors of velours, silk damask or brocatelle. Has spring seat, and back is richly hand embroidered. Comfortable and artistic. Weight, 40 pounds.

Grade,	G	H	K
Price	$14.20	$14.85	$15.45

$50-$75

No. 446. A beautiful hall or reception chair. High back, handsomely carved and polished; strong and comfortable. Has the saddle wood seat and French legs. Veneered mahogany and natural curly birch. Weight, 12 pounds.
Price, only.......................$5.75

$50-$75

No. 481W. A saddle wood seat parlor rocker. Strong and comfortable. Beautifully polished and mahogany veneer inlaid back. Can furnish this in natural birch or mahogany finish Weight, 27 lbs.
Price, only...................... $5.25

$55-$75

Odd Pieces for the Parlor

No. 832½ W. Parlor Rocker. Saddle wood seat with high arms; carved back. Comfortable and strong and very stylish. Made of quartered oak or birch Antique. finish. Weight, 20 pounds.
Green or mahogany finish, only....$7.50
Chair to match above, only........ 6.50

$50-$75

No. 800 Fancy Odd Chair, for parlor or hall. Handsome design and very artistic. Mahogany veneered back, hand carved and highly polished. Weight 11 pounds. In mahogany finish only.
Price........................ ....$3.85

$25-$45

No. 426. A perfect parlor rocker. Has the shaped saddle wood seat. Made of mahogany and birch and finished only in mahogany. Beautifully carved, polished and back is richly inlaid. Would grace the finest parlors. Weight, 30 pounds.
Price, in mahogany............ ...$11.00

$50-$75

No. 804. A reception or parlor chair, with spring seat and embroidered back. Upholstered in a fine quality of imported plush. Artistic and refined design. Mahogany finish. Weight, 12 pounds.
Price, each................. ......$7.00

$40-$50

4

Odd Pieces for the Parlor

No. 472½ W. Ladies' Parlor Rocker.
Made of solid mahogany, richly carved and polished, and perfectly inlaid with pearl and holly. Shaped saddle wood seat. Strong and comfortable. Weight, 14 pounds.
Price..............................$9.75
Chair to match above, in solid mahogany, only...............................$9.00

$30-$50

No. 837 Parlor Rocker. Beautifully made, with solid mahogany back, richly inlaid. Has full upholstered seat in all colors of silk damask. Finished in mahogany only. Weight, 27 pounds.
Price............... ....$12.25

$60-$75

No. 2737 English Reading Chair. Made of natural birch or imitation mahogany. Has extra high back and spring seat. Very comfortable and artistic. Back is beautifully embroidered. Send for samples.

Grade,	G	H	K
Price	$10.10	$11.20	$12.25

$60-$80

No. 757W. A perfect beauty in a saddle wood seat or leather seat, with all full twisted spindles; carved and polished. Made of birch and mahogany. Finished mahogany. Weight, 27 pounds.
Saddle wood seat....................$5.25
Cobbler leather seat................ 5.50

$60-$75

Odd Pieces for the Parlor or Hall

No. 2753 Roman Chair. Made of oak or natural birch and mahogany finish and nicely polished; seat is covered with silk damask, brocatelle or tapestry; very ornamental and pretty. Weight, 10 pounds.
Price, only.............................$1.95

$25-$45

No. 2732 Chair. Made of birch, mahogany finish. Has spring seat, and is a very artistic piece. The most desirable covering is our velours under grade G and H. Comfortable and well made; back is richly embroidered.

Grade,	F	G	H	K
Price	$8.90	$9.25	$10.30	$11.70

$50-$75

No. 2163 Roman Chair. Very ornamental and quite comfortable. Made of light curly birch or imitation mahogany, beautifully hand carved and highly polished. A very artistic piece for a parlor; makes a nice window or corner chair; is also pretty with a pillow or cushion.
Price, only...................... ....$4.20
Price, without back.......................3.50

$40-$60

No. 2560 Parlor Chair. Made of solid mahogany, carved and highly polished. Has a large spring seat; sides and back nicely upholstered and well padded, making it exceedingly comfortable. A very artistic and refined design. Weight, 40 pounds. Back and sides richly embroidered.

Grade,	G	H	K
Price	$23.60	$24.95	$27.50

$60-$80

Odd Pieces for the Parlor or Hall

No. 470 W. A ladies' desk, hall, chamber or parlor chair; wood or cane seat. Made of oak, mahogany finish, natural birch or white maple. A gem for the money. Weight, 14 lbs.
Price.....................$2.65
Rocker, to match above, only. 3.25

$50-$75

No. 489 Roman Chair. Without back. A very shapely pattern; the lines are perfect. Made of oak or birch and finished in antique or mahogany finish. The mahogany is veneered with solid mahogany. Weight, 12 pounds.
Price, each.................$4.50

$40-$60

No. 2758 Fancy Odd Chair for Parlor. Made of birch, finished mahogany, carved and polished; has high arms, shaped back and large spring seat. Weight, 30 pounds. Seat covered with the finest of silk damask.
Price.....................$10.25

$40-$60

No. 449½ W. A ladies' parlor or bedroom rocker; highly polished and carved; has full twist spindles; strong and comfortable. Natural birch or mahogany finish. Weight, 12 pounds.
Price....................$4.25
Chair to match above, suitable
  for all purposes, only.......3.25

$75-$100

Odd Pieces for the Parlor or Hall

No. 2735 Parlor Chair. Back is richly hand-embroidered and frame is highly polished. Made of birch, finished mahogany; has shaped back and large spring seat. Weight, 30 pounds.

Grade,   **G**   **H**   **K**

Price.................$9 80 $10.80 $11.85

$50-$75

No. 2759 Fancy Parlor Chair. Frame is made of solid mahogany, hand carved and beautifully polished; back is shaped and has high arms which makes it very comfortable. Has a large spring seat, covered with silk damask. Weight, 35 pounds. Send for samples.

Price, in K silk damask. $10.80

$40-$60

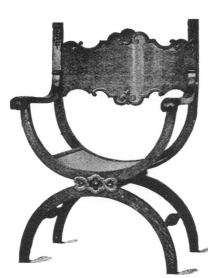

No. 490 Roman Chair. Handsome carved design, very shapely. The proper thing for odd parlor or window piece; also for hall use. Quartered oak or mahogany finish. Weight, 18 pounds.

Price.............................$8.00

$50-$75

No. 445 Reception or Parlor Chair. Has French legs and a saddle wood seat. Back is upholstered with figured velour plush, hand carved and highly hand-finished. Natural birch, mahogany finish or quartered oak. Weight, 15 pounds.

Price.................$6 25

$65-$80

8

Large Comfortable Chairs and Rockers
For Library, Parlor or Sitting Room

No. 2 Students' Chair. A very popular design at a very low figure. Frame is made of oak, and the proper covering for this chair is our grade F Kaiser plush or corduroy. Richly tufted, and a good heavy frame. Exceedingly comfortable. Makes a fine reading chair. Weight, 50 lbs.

	Grade,	E	F	G	H
Price		$4.90	$8.40	$9.80	$11.20

$50-$75

No. 408 Morris Reclining Chair. Nothing more comfortable on the market. Works very simple. With a brass rod at the back, it can be adjusted to any angle. Frame is made of oak, highly polished. Has extra large, heavy, thick, loose cushions for seat and back. Nothing made in the way of chairs begins to approach this for luxury and positive ease. Weight, about 45 lbs. Cushion covered with a good grade of corduroy.

Price in corduroy, only $7.80
Price in figured tapestry, only 6.30

$50-$75

No. 2781 Turkish Chair. Frame is made of quartered oak or mahogany finish, and polished. Spring seat, back and edges. Very large and roomy. The filling consists of the finest moss, hair and steel springs. Height, 39 inches; width between arms, 20 inches. Will guarantee it for comfort. When made in leather is trimmed with large leather tacks. Weight, 75 lbs.

Grade F, Corduroy or Kaiser Plush $16.55
" G 17.55
" H 19.90
Leather 20.50
   Rocker to match, $1.00 extra.

$50-$75

No. 2481 Turkish Chair. Frame is made of quartered oak or mahogany finish, carved, and polished like a mirror. Spring seat, back and edges. Very large and roomy. The filling consists of the finest moss, hair and steel springs. Height, 39 inches; width between arms, 20 inches. Fine enough for any library or home. Weight, 75 lbs.

	Grade,	F	G	H	L	Leather
Price		$22.75	$24.05	$25.35	$29.50	$29.25

Rocker to match above, $1.00 extra.

$70-$90

Large Comfortable Chairs and Rockers
For Library, Parlor or Sitting Room

No. 2767 Turkish Rocker. Here is the cheapest Turkish rocker on the market. Back and arms are richly tufted. Has large seat and high back, spring seat, back and arms, made of the finest leather, springs, hair and moss, and trimmed with leather fringe and large leather tacks. One of the most comfortable rockers in our store. Weight, 50 lbs.

Grade F, Corduroy or Kaiser Plush $23.60
Leather, with fringe 29.70
Grade G 24.30
   " H 25.65
   " K 27.65
    Chair to match above, $1.00 less.

$80-$110

No. 1725 Turkish Rocker. The filling consists of the finest hair and best steel springs. Upholstered with genuine leather and richly trimmed with beautiful leather fringe and large leather tacks. Nothing more comfortable made. Is extra well padded, and has large spring seat, back and arms.

Price, in leather..$45.50
Grade F 33.75
   " G 35.90
   " H 36.45

$100-$125

No. 2461 Turkish Rocker. The filling consists of the finest hair and best steel springs. Upholstered in genuine leather, richly trimmed with beautiful leather fringe. Send for samples. Nothing more comfortable made. A rich and elegant design.

Price, in Leather.................$30.35   Grade G $25.05
Grade F, Corduroy or Kaiser Plush. 23.60   Grade H.............. 26.00
    Chair to match above, $1.00 less.

$115-$140

No. 2773 Turkish Rocker. Extra well padded and contains the finest of steel springs, hair and moss. Can furnish it in all colors of leather and other coverings. Trimmed with beautiful leather fringe and large leather tacks. Samples mailed free. Weight, 60 lbs.

	Grade,	F	G	H	Leather
Price		$27.00	$28.50	$29.70	$33.00

    Chair to match above, $1.00 less.

$115-$150

Fancy Parlor or Sitting Room Rockers

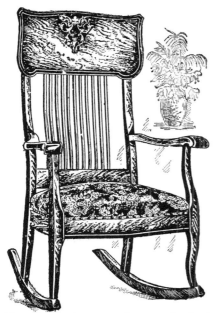

No. 936. Here is a pretty and ornamental rocker for parlor. Made of curly birch, finished mahogany, and back is beautifully inlaid and polished like a piano. Spring seat is covered with the finest silk damask or brocatelle. This is extra high grade. Weight, 40 lbs. Price...$6.95

$65-$85

No. 609 Large Arm Rocker. Made of solid mahogany and highly hand polished, and back is beautifully inlaid. Has a shaped wood seat, highly polished. Very comfortable, refined and artistic. Weight, 25 pounds.
Price, in solid mahogany.....................$8.40

$65-$90

No. 935 Large Arm Rocker. Made of quarter-sawed oak, richly hand carved and highly polished, and has French legs and back is extra high. Is extra large and made of very heavy stock. Has a large spring seat upholstered with silk brocatelle or tapestry. Is worth double our price. Very massive and a rich design. Weight, about 40 lbs.
Price, only...................................$5.25

$85-$110

No. 626. This is an extra fine rocker. Made of birch finished mahogany, richly hand carved and polished like a piano. The stock used in this rocker is select and beautiful. Height of back, 25 inches; width, 20 inches. Has the cobbler sole leather seat. Very comfortable Weight, 20 lbs.
Price, only...................................$7.45

$65-$80

Fancy Parlor or Sitting Room Rockers

No. 940C Rocker. This beautiful French rocker is made of quatered oak and polished like a piano. Has rope spindles and posts, which gives it a rich appearance. The stock in this rocker is very select and beautiful. Has French legs and heavy large arms. Weight, 20 lbs. Price, only...$4.90

$75-$110

No. 625 Rocker. This is one of the most artistic rockers in our stock, and is also one of the most comfortable. Made of beautiful select birch finished mahogany (the grain is about as handsome as solid mahogany) hand carved and polished like a mirror. The design is beautiful and an ornament to any room. Well braced and very strong. Just the thing for your parlor, and would also make a very pretty present. Price, only...$6.95

$60-$85

No. 933 Rocker. This beautiful large arm rocker is made of quarter-sawed oak and polished like a piano. Is very large and heavy. Has a very high back and large spring seat, upholstered with silk tapestry or plush. We especially recommend this for solid comfort. Weight, 50 lbs.
Price...$5.60

$65-$80

No. 671 Rocker. Something new in a saddle wood seat parlor and library arm rocker. Extremely handsome. Made of solid mahogany, with fine carving and inlaid work in the back. Will grace the finest furnished homes in the country. Hand polished, and has the artistic rope spindles.
Price, only.................................$12.75

$75-$100

Fancy Parlor or Sitting Room Rockers

No. 932 Arm Rocker. Solid quarter-sawed oak, polished like a piano. Seat is covered with silk damask. This is extra fine and very ornamental. Weight, 20 lbs. Excellent value for the money asked.
Price, only..................................$4.55

$90-$125

No. 926C. A great bargain. Fine parlor or sitting-room ladies' or gentlemen's arm chair. Perfect comfort. Made of quarter-sawed oak, with cobbler embossed sole leather shoemaker's seat. No wearing out of plush or tapestry on this rocker, and just as handsome. Back is extra high and comfortable. Weight, 18 lbs. Retail price, $6.00.
Our price, only................................$3.95

$90-$125

585

No. 585. A beautiful parlor rocker for ladies. Made of select birch and finished mahogany and highly hand polished. Has the cobbler seat made of sole leather, embossed. The wood used in this rocker is beautiful, and must be seen to be appreciated; has the rope spindles, which are very pretty. Weight, 17 lbs. This rocker is made with spindles under the arms.
Price, only.............................$5.95

$90-$110

No. 940 Large Arm Rocker. Made of quarter-sawed oak, richly hand carved and highly polished. is extra large and made of very heavy stock. Has a large spring seat upholstered with silk brocatelle or tapestry. Is worth double our price. Very massive and a rich design; also has the rope spindles and posts, and French legs, which are very pretty and artistic. Weight, about 40 lbs.
Price, only.............................$5.75

$90-$125

Fancy Parlor or Sitting Room Rockers

No. 926 Rocker. A beautiful, large rocker. Solid oak, highly polished. Back is very high, and spring seat covered with silk plush or tapestry. Good value. This is one of our best and most ornamental styles. Weight, 25 pounds. Retails for double our price.
Price, only....................................$4.90

No. 930C Large Arm Rocker. Made of quarter-sawed oak, neatly carved and highly polished. Has the leather seat, which is comfortable and durable. Has a very high back. Weight, 18 lbs. Good value.
Price, only....................................$3.90

$90-$110

No. 687 Large Arm Rocker. For parlor or sitting-room. Made of quarter-sawed oak or mahogany finish, hand carved and highly polished. Has sole leather seat. This rocker also contains ornamental rope spindles and posts; is made of extra heavy and fine stock, and is worth nearly double our price. Weight, 22 pounds.
Price, only....................................$4.95

No. 597. A beautful parlor rocker. Made of birch and finished mahogany, richly carved and highly hand polished. Has the polished wood seat. The wood used in this rocker is beautiful, and must be seen to be appreciated. Weight, 20 pounds. This rocker has the rope spindles.
Price..$6.85

$60-$90

Fancy Parlor or Sitting Room Rockers

No. 930 Large Arm Rocker. Made of quarter-sawed oak, carved and polished. Has high back and extra large spring seat covered with silk plush or tapestry. Very comfortable and cheap. Weight, 20 lbs. Price, only.....................................$4.45

No. 535. A very beautiful rocker. Made of quarter-sawed oak or mahogany finish, neatly carved and highly polished. Has the rope spindles and posts, which are exceedingly artistic and ornamental. Back is high, and has large spring seat covered in brocatelle or tapestry. The stock is beautiful; a good design. Weight, 20 pounds. Price, only.....................................$3.55

$75-$100

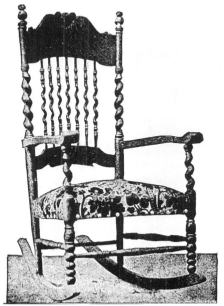

No. 925 Rocker. New design and very orna-mental. Price is very low. Made of quarter-sawed oak, neatly carved and highly polished. Back is high, and has large spring seat covered in plush or tapestry. The stock is beautiful. A good design. Weight, 20 lbs. Price, only.....................................$3.85

No. 536 Rocker. A beautiful, large rocker for little money. The rope effect which it contains in the spindles and posts gives it a very rich and artistic appearance. Solid oak or mahogany finish, highly polished. Back is very high, and spring seat covered with silk tapestry or brocatelle; good value. This is one of our best and most ornamental styles. Weight, 25 pounds. Price, only.....................................$5.00

$75-$100

15

Fancy Parlor or Sitting Room Rockers

No. 927 Ladies' Extra High Back Rocker.
Made of quarter-sawed oak, carved and highly polished. Seat is covered with a fine grade of silk plush or tapestry. Has a fine spring seat and is very comfortable. Weight, 18 pounds. A bargain.
Price, only..................................$2.55

No. 956C Extra High Back Arm Rocker. Well made of solid oak, carved and highly polished. Has the cobbler seat made of sole leather. Very large and good value. Satisfaction guaranteed. Weight, 18 lbs.
Price, only................. ....$2.85

$50-$75

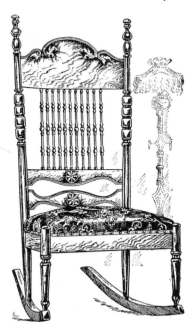

No. 929 Ladies' Fancy Rocker. Made of quarter-sawed oak, highly hand polished and carved. Back is extra high, and has large spring seat, covered with silk plush or tapestry. A beauty for the money. Weight, 18 pounds.
Price, only...................... ....$3.45

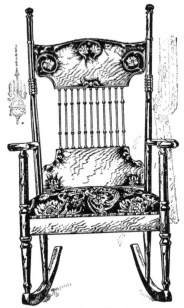

No. 928 Arm Rocker. How is this for a bargain? A large arm rocker, made of solid oak and highly polished. Spring seat is covered with a good grade of plush or tapestry. This is the best and cheapest rocker in America for the money. Comfortable and ornamental.
Price, only...................................$3.85

$70-$100

16

Fancy Rockers

No. 460 Parlor Rocker. Suitable for any parlor. With saddle wood seat; French legs, all bolted to the seat. Has high shaped and carved arms. Beautifully carved and inlaid back. Piano finished. Made of birch and finished mahogany or natural curly birch. The grain is handsomer than solid mahogany. Weight, 20 lbs.

Price, only $11.10

$50-$70

No. 835 Parlor Rocker. A fine Flemish design, made of oak and finished antique, Flemish finish or malechite. Has rope turnings and elegant heavy hand-carved back, with fine silk damask spring seat. The latest design on the market. Very comfortable and strong. No finer made. Weight, 20 lbs.

Price, ... $12.00

$90-$115

No. 486W A Parlor Rocker. Made only in saddle wood seat, and highly hand polished. Something very graceful in finish, with an elegant design of real inlaid work in the back. A beautiful and artistic pattern. Weight, 18 lbs. Made of birch and mahogany and finished in mahogany.

Price, only $7.25

$70-$90

No. 478B A Parlor Upholstered Rocker. This is a beautiful piece of furniture and an ornament to any room. Seat is covered in all colors of silk damask. Spring seat. Handsomely inlaid with the best design. Is made of birch and mahogany, and when finished in mahogany it looks like the genuine wood. Can be had in natural curly birch also. Usually sells for $17.00.

Our price is only $11.00

$90-$120

Fancy Rockers

No. 2057 Fancy Rocker. Made of maple, finished mahogany. Has leather seat, and a pretty design of imitation marqueterie on the back. High arms, rodded to seat. Very showy, ornamental and cheap. Highly polished, and a beauty for the money. Weight, 15 lbs.
Price...$3.25

$50-$70

No. 467 Parlor Rocker. Made of oak or birch, highly polished; finished in malechite, antique, natural birch or mahogany finish. The mahogany finish is perfect, as the rocker is veneered with real mahogany before finishing. We can recommend it for comfort and durability.
No. 467W, saddle wood seat, only.............$4.00
No. 467, cobbler leather seat, only............. 4.25

$45-$55

No. 735 Fancy Rocker. This is the best and most showy leather seat rocker on the market for the money. Very showy, and has large, high back. Is very comfortable and strong. Made of hard wood and finished mahogany or antique. Extra good value. Weight, 16 lbs.
Price, each.................................$ 1.95
Two or more packed together per dozen 23.00

$50-$70

No. 482W A Pretty Saddle Wood Seat Parlor or Sitting Room Rocker. Strong, showy and comfortable. A handsome design, made of oak or birch, finished antique or mahogany, and highly polished. The mahogany finish is mahogany veneer. Weight, 16 lbs.
Price, only...................................$4.50

$50-$70

Fancy Rockers

No. 840B Ladies' Slipper or Low-back Rocker.
Made of oak or birch, polished. Upholstered seat
and back, with all colors of figured plush. Very pretty
and comfortable, and when finished in malechite,
with colors to harmonize, is perfectly charming.
Weight, 15 lbs.
Price, only..................................$4.25

$50-$60

No. 2023A Misses' Cobbler Seat Rocker.
Made of maple, finished mahogany, highly polished.
Has genuine leather seat, with handsome design of
imitation marqueterie on the back. This is a beauty,
and large enough for a small lady.
Price, only..................................$2.65

$50-$70

No. 2056 Leather Seat Rocker. Made of maple
and finished mahogany, with an elaborate design of
marqueterie on the back. Has high arms, rodded to
seat. Very attractive. Large, roomy, strong and
comfortable. Weight, 18 lbs.
Price, only..................................$2.65

$50-$75

**No. 404BL Leather Seat and Back Parlor
Rocker.** Made of oak, highly polished. High arms,
well braced and richly carved. This is most attractive
and pretty when upholstered in apple green or red
leather. Can furnish in all colors of leather. Weight,
18 lbs.
Price, only..................................$4.25

$50-$75

Reed and Rattan Goods

No. 2952 Ottoman. This is a very attractive ottoman, made of the best reed, well braced. Very useful and ornamental. Height, 15 inches; size of top, 16x16 inches. Weight, 7 lbs.

Natural reed $3.35
Shellac finish 4.00
White and gold or all gold. 5.60

$20-$25

No. 2951 Jardiniere Stand. Something very showy and makes a nice flower stand. Finished wood top, hexagon shape. Made strong, of reed, well braced. Weight, 7 lbs.

Natural reed $3.55
Shellac finish 4.20
White and gold or all gold. 5.80
Height, 21 inches; size of top, 13x13 inches.

$30-$40

No. 2953A Fancy Parlor Chair or Window Seat. Made of fine reed, well braced, and has full basket seat. Very stylish and artistic. Every one has a place for a piece of this kind. Weight, 9 lbs.

Natural reed $4.45
Shellac finish. 5.35
White and gold or all gold. 7.30

$30-$50

No. 4667A. Something new. One of the latest things in reception or parlor chairs. Has a fine shape, which makes it very comfortable. Furnished only in shellac. Made of fine reed, and in addition has just enough daintily colored reeds woven in to make it very attractive. A beauty. Weight, 10 lbs. Price, in shellac finish, only. $7.10

$70-$90

No. 2943A Fancy Reception Chair. Made of all reed, cane seat. Very appropriate for reception hall or parlor. Ornamental and well made.

Natural reed $4.45
Shellac finish. 5.35
Enameled white and gold or all gold 7.35

$80-$100

No. 4670A. This is a very handsome reed arm chair. All fine work, artistically woven with daintily colored reeds. Very pretty, and one of the latest things out. Strong and comfortable. Weight, 9 lbs. Price, in shellac finish, only. $9.00

$80-$100

Reed and Rattan Goods

No. 2942E Parlor or Corner Chair.
Very handsome, especially when finished in white and gold or all gold. Is light in appearance, still it is made strong, and is very attractive. Weight, 10 lbs.
Natural reed $4.45
Shellac finish....................... 5.35
White and gold or all gold......... 7.30

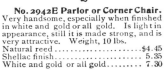

$80-$100

No. 2907A. An exceedingly handsome hall or reception room chair. If you want an attractive, odd chair for your parlor, this will be the proper thing. Weight, 10 lbs.
Natural reed $5.35
Shellac finish................ 6.25
Enameled white and gold or all gold 8.25

$80-$100

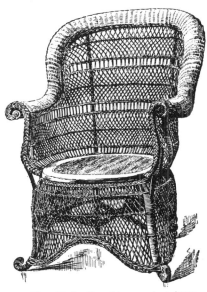

No. 4660C. Something new in a fancy and comfortable arm chair. Pretty and handsome design. Made of the best reed. Strong and artistic. Weight, 14 lbs.
Price, in shellac finish $9.35

$60-$80

No. 2893D Large Arm Reed Rocker.
Examine the great amount of work on it. Very large and high back, fancy arms and base. A fine ornament for any house. If you want something fine and very showy, order this. Weight, 18 lbs. Height of back from seat, 32 inches.
Natural reed $7.55
Shellac finish............................ 8.45

$100-$125

Reed and Rattan Goods

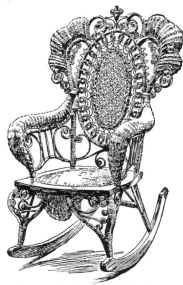

No. 2934B Ladies' Parlor Rocker.
Showy and attractive design. The fluted
reed effect on the sides are attractive and
pretty. Made of the best quality of reed, and
a great deal of work on it. Will surely please
any lady. Has cane seat. Weight, 19 lbs.
Price in natural reed....................$7.10
Price in shellac finish.................. 8.00

$100-$125

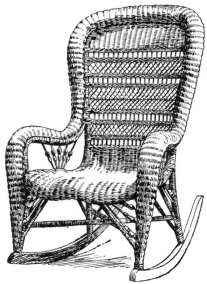

No. 2782D Large Comfort Rocker. Made of
the best reeds, finely woven. Very comfortable, and
will last a lifetime. It pays to buy the best. Back
high enough to rest the head on. Weight 19 lbs.
2782B, Ladies' size, natural reed, only..........$6.25
2782B, Ladies' size, shellac finish, only 7.10
2782D, Gents' size, natural reed, only........... 8.00
2782D, Gents' size, shellac finish, only.......... 8.85

$60-$75

No. 4656B. Something entirely new. A very
odd yet taking design. Has the finely woven basket
seat, strong and very attractive. We will guarantee
this for solid comfort. Weight, 18 lbs.
4656B, Ladies' size, natural reed..............$ 7.00
4356B, Ladies' size, shellac finish. 8.00
4656D, Gents' size, natural reed............... 9.35
4656D, Gents' size, shellac finish 10.50

$50-$75

No. 2852D. Here is a still finer gents' reed
rocker. Just as comfortable as it can be. Large
and very strong. Will give good service for ten
years. Difficult to find any better than this.
Weight, 18 lbs.

Natural reed $8.00
Shellac finish........... .... 8.85

$90-$120

Parlor Suits

$110-$150

$90-$110

$100-$130

$30-$50

$50-$60

No. 2566 Parlor Suit. Made of quarter-sawed oak or imitation mahogany, beautifully hand carved and highly hand polished. Backs are biscuit tufted. Large, heavy frame, with French legs. Has spring seats and edges. Nothing but the very finest of coverings and materials used in this suit. Length of sofa, 48 inches. Weight, 220 pounds. The parlor chairs of this suit are very artistic and pretty.

Grade	F	G	H	K	L
Sofa	$ 6.75	$ 7.55	$ 8.80	$10.15	$11.15
Arm Chair	3.40	4.00	4.20	4.40	5 75
Rocker	5.05	5.70	6.10	7.10	7.40
Divan	5.05	5.90	6.40	7.40	8.10
Two Parlor Chairs	4.00	4.60	5.00	5.40	6.10
Suit complete, 6 pieces	$24.25	$27.75	$30.50	$34.45	$38.50

Parlor Suits

$175-$225

$115-$130

$115-$130

$50-$60

$75-$85

No. 2541½ Parlor Suit. Very artistic and rich design, with brackets under the arms and French legs. Made of solid oak or imitation mahogany, hand carved and highly hand polished. Richly upholstered with fine silk damask, tapestry or brocatelle. Backs are richly biscuit tufted. Has large spring seats and edges, trimmed with silk plush and extra heavy arms well braced. Length of sofa, 48 inches; length of divan, 35 inches. Weight, 220 pounds. Good value and cheap.

Grade,	F	G	H	L
Sofa	$ 7.00	$ 8.05	$ 9.10	$11.20
Arm Chair	3.60	3.85	4.20	5.85
Rocker	5.25	5.75	6.15	7.70
Divan	5.05	5.65	6.30	8.40
Two Parlor Chairs	4.30	4.70	5.10	6.00
Suit complete, 6 pieces	$25.20	$28.00	$30.85	$39.15

Parlor Suits

$140-$180

$125-$150

$100-$125

$40-$50

$60-$75

No. 2816 Parlor Suit. Frame is made of quarter-sawed oak or mahogany finish, hand carved and highly hand polished. This is one of the most ornamental suits we have. Pretty French legs and large arms, well braced. Backs are very showy and pretty. Spring seats and edges. Trimmed in silk plush if desired; samples mailed free. The divan is exceedingly ornamental and good size for a small parlor. Length of divan, 37 inches; length of sofa, 48 inches. Weight, 220 lbs.

Grade	F	G	H	L	P
Sofa	$6.90	$7.40	$7.75	$9.45	$10.15
Arm Chair	3.50	3.85	4.05	4.40	4.75
Rocker	5.20	5.55	5.75	6.10	7.10
Divan	5.20	5.75	6.10	6.75	7.75
Two Parlor Chairs	4.20	4.50	4.70	5.10	5.40
Suit complete, 6 pieces	$25.00	$27.05	$28.35	$31.80	$35.15

Parlor Suits

$200-$230

$90-$110

$125-$150

$50-$75

$75-$90

No. 2815 Parlor Suit. Here is an extra heavy weight suit for little money. Made of quartered oak or mahogany finish, carved and highly polished. Large braces under the arms. Has spring seats and edges, and trimmed in silk plush if desired. Extra large and well made. Samples of covering mailed free. We will separate any of our parlor suits. Weight, 220 lbs. Suit consists of 6 pieces.

Grade,	F	G	H	L	P
Sofa	$8.75	$9.05	$9.45	$10.50	$11.50
Arm Chair	4.05	4.25	4.35	5.75	5.85
Rocker	6.00	6.30	6.55	7.45	8.10
Divan	6.10	6.50	6.90	7.80	8.75
Two Parlor Chairs	4.90	5.00	5.20	5.70	6.40
Suit complete, 6 pieces	$29.80	$31.10	$32.45	$37.20	$40.60

$200-$250

$75-$90

$90-$115

Grade,	G	H	K	L
Sofa	$12 15	$12.49	$13.16	$13.84
Arm Chair	8.77	9.45	10.13	10.80
Parlor Chair	4.72	5.06	5.74	6.41
Suit complete, 3 pieces	$25.64	$26.90	$29.03	$31.05

No. 2800½ Suit. This beautiful French design is made of select birch, finished mahogany, highly hand polished. Has spring seats, and upholstered in the finest damask, tapestry, brocatelle or silk plush. Has large, comfortable spring seats. Weight, 125 pounds. Send for samples (free). Suit consists of sofa, arm chair and parlor chair. Nothing more artistic made than above suit. Backs are beautifully hand embroidered.

We can furnish above suit without embroidery for $2.00 less.

Parlor Suits

$125-$150

$30-$50

$75-$100

Grade,	G	H	K	L
Sofa	$15.52	$16.20	$17.55	$19.58
Arm Chair	10.80	11.14	11.81	12.83
Parlor Chair	6.08	6.41	7.09	7.76
Suit complete, 3 pieces	$32.40	$33.75	$36.45	$40.17

No. 2734½ Reception or Parlor Suit. Made of birch and finished mahogany, highly hand polished. Is exceedingly comfortable, as all pieces have shaped backs. The most desirable covering is corduroy or silk plush, as the backs are beautifully hand embroidered. Samples mailed free upon request. An exceedingly artistic and refined design. Weight, about 150 pounds. Seats contain the best of springs and are well filled. We sell separate pieces if desired.

We can furnish above suit without embroidery for $2.50 less.

Two-Piece Parlor or Library Suits

$150-$175

$85-$125

Grade,	G	H	K	L
Sofa	$16.88	$17.55	$18.90	$21.60
Arm Chair	12.83	13.50	14.18	15.53
Suit complete, 2 pieces	$29.71	$31.05	$33.08	$37.13

No. 2722½ Parlor or Reception Suit. Made of solid mahogany with inlaid lines, and backs are all beautifully hand embroidered. The frames are richly shaped, which makes them very comfortable, seats are large and well filled and contain the best of springs. The most desirable covering is wide ribbed corduroy or silk plush, as the embroidery looks much handsomer in plain colors. Length of sofa, 45 inches. Suit consists of sofa and arm chair. Send for samples, mailed free. Weight, 125 pounds.

Two-Piece Parlor or Library Suits

$250-$300

$175-$200

Grade,	H	K	L	P
Sofa	$47.25	$48 60	$51.30	$54.00
Arm Chair	31.05	35.10	36.45	37.80
Suit complete, 2 pieces	$78.30	$83.70	$87.75	$91.80

No. 2812 Parlor, Library or Reception Suit. Made of the most select mahogany, hand polished and carved by expert carvers. The sides, back and seat are upholstered with the finest of silk damask and imported coverings. Seats are extra large, well filled and made especially for comfort. If you want something artistic handsome and massive, this will surely please you. Weight, 140 pounds. Length of sofa, 51 inches; width of chair, 36 inches. Samples of coverings mailed free, upon request.

Parlor Suits, Over-Stuffed

$100-$150

$50-$75

$100-$115

Grade,	E	F	ɑ	H	K	L
Sofa........................	$6.35	$7.10	$7.45	$8.10	$9.15	$10.15
Arm Chair	4.05	4.85	5.30	5.40	6.10	6.75
Ladies' Arm Chair.........	3.50	4.05	4.35	4.40	4.75	6.10
Two Parlor Chairs.........	3.70	4.10	4.60	5.80	7.10	8.40
Suit complete, 5 pieces..	$17.60	$20.10	$21.70	$23.70	$27.10	$31.40

No. 2529½ Parlor Suit. This beautiful parlor suit is upholstered with silk damask, broca-telle or the finest silk tapestry, and trimmed with good heavy fringe. Has large spring seats and edges. Filling consists of the best moss and fine steel springs. Suit consists of sofa, rocker, arm chair, two parlor chairs. Length of sofa, 55 inches. We guarantee satisfaction on this suit, and can be returned at our expense if not satisfactory. Weight 200 lbs.

Parlor Suits

$150-$175

$90-$115

$115-$130

Grade,	H	K	L	P
Sofa	$24.30	$25.31	$27.00	$27.68
Arm Chair	16.88	17.21	17.89	18.90
Rocker	17.55	17.89	18.56	19.58
Parlor Chair	11.14	11.81	12.15	12.83
Parlor Chair	11.14	11.81	12.15	12.83
Suit complete, 5 pieces	$81.01	$84.03	$87.75	$91.82

No. 2543 Turkish Parlor Suit. This elegant suit is filled with excellent long hair and moss, and the springs are of the finest steel. Is all spring seats and backs. Nothing more comfortable can be made. The very best of material is used throughout. The upholstering is the finest imported damask, brocatelle or silk tapestry. Seats are large and exceedingly comfortable. The fringe is of the choicest silk and extends all around. . The backs are the same as seat covering. Length of sofa, 58 inches. Send for samples; mailed free upon request. Weight, 200 pounds. Rich and refined.

Above suit with wool fringe in place of silk fringe, $5.00 less.

Couches

No. 2263 Couch. Nicely tufted, and covered with a good grade of corduroy or Kaiser plush. (Send for samples.) Filling consists of moss and best steel springs. Length, 6 feet 5 inches; width, 26 inches. Good size and exceedingly comfortable. There is nothing nicer than a good, comfortable couch for a sitting-room. Nicely trimmed in a good grade of fringe to match covering. We are sure this will please you, and can be returned at our expense if not as represented. Weight, 80 lbs. Spring edges.
Grade F crushed plush, Kaiser plush or corduroy..$5.75

$90-$110

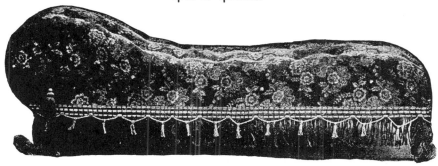

No. 2291 Tufted Couch. Is upholstered with fine corduroy, Kaiser plush or tapestry. Just the right shape to be exceedingly comfortable. Good size. Width, 27 inches; length, 79 inches. Trimmed with a fine grade of fringe, which extends all around the couch. Nothing but the best springs and moss used in this couch. A bargain at our price. Weight, 80 lbs. Hard edge.

Grade F covering, only......................$ 7.70	Crushed plush...............................$9.00
	Cretonne.................................... 4.90

$110-$130

No. 1408½ Couch. Nicely tufted, and covered with a good grade of corduroy or Kaiser plush. (Send for samples.) Filling consists of moss and best steel springs. Length, 6 feet 6 inches; width, 30 inches. Good size and exceedingly comfortable. Nicely trimmed in a good grade of fringe to match covering. We are sure this will please you, and can be returned at our expense if not as represented. Weight, 80 lbs. Spring edges.

Grade F crushed plush, Kaiser plush or corduroy $10.50	Grade H................................. ....$14.30
Grade G 12.35	Pantasote 16.00
	Genuine Leather............................ 22.75

$90-$115

Couches

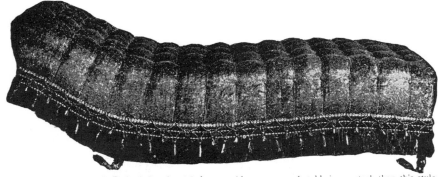

No. 2290 Turkish Tufted Couch. We have nothing more comfortable in our stock than this style. Beautifully fringed all around, also under head and foot. Upholstered with an extra grade of corduroy, Kaiser plush or tapestry. (Send for sample.) The very finest of material used on the inside of couch. We guarantee satisfaction in every way, and can be returned at our expense if not satisfactory. This is also very ornamental, as it is a piece of art in this line. Weight, 85 lbs.

Grade F covering...........................$11.85
Grade G covering........................... 14.00

Grade H covering...........................$17.00
Pantasote................................... 21.00
Leather................................... 29.90

$175-$200

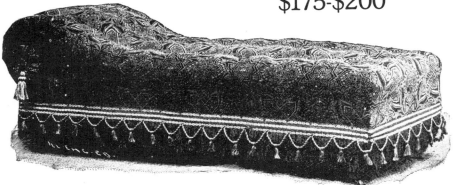

No. 52½ Hygienic Couch. Full spring edge. Width, 26 inches; length, 6 feet. Has 38 springs, with woven wire top and bottom. Spring structure is open to view and admission of light and air. Upholstered in heavy wide wale corduroy or velours. (Send for samples.) Springs guaranteed never to come through upholstered top. Weight, 90 lbs.

Price, in corduroy or Kaiser plush, only...$6.95

$125-$150

ACME HYGIENIC COUCH

No. 83 Hygienic Couch. Full spring edge. Width, 30 inches; length, 6 feet 6 inches. Has 55 steel springs, with woven wire top and bottom. Spring structure is open to view and admission of light and air. Covered with the finest of corduroy or Kaiser plush. Exceedingly comfortable and extra well made. Weight, 100 lbs.

Price, in corduroy or Kaiser plush...$15.15

$175-$200

Bed Lounges

No. 2243 Bed Lounge. A good, heavy framed lounge, made of quartered oak, carved and highly polished. Width when open, 48 inches; length, 6 feet. Is nicely trimmed with corduroy or silk plush. Has a woven wire spring bed with a cotton top mattress. Back is extra high and comfortable. Good design and size. A bargain at our price.

Brussels carpet............$ 9.95   Grade E.................$10.65   Grade G................$12.65
Velvet carpet............. 11.25   Grade F................. 11.25   Grade H................. 13.95

$200-$250

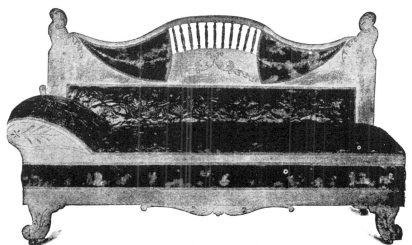

No. 1232 Bed Lounge. Oak frame, polished and carved. Length, 6 feet; width when open, 49 inches. This is a very large and heavy frame. Has a woven wire spring bed with a cotton top mattress. Back is richly trimmed in silk plush. Retails for almost double our price. Weight, 125 lbs. The most desirable covering for this lounge is our grades F or H corduroy.

Brussels carpet............$10.70   Velvet carpet.............$11.95   Grade F................$11.95
Grade G ....$13.55   Grade H.................................. 14.95

$175-$215

Bed Lounges

No. 2266 Bed Lounge. This is one of our new styles, and a design that is sure to please. Made of quarter-sawed oak, carved and polished. Corduroy is the most durable covering for this. Length, 6 feet; width, when open, 50 inches. Has a woven wire bed and a cotton top mattress. Weight, 130 lbs. Extra good value.

Brussels carpet............$11.45   Velvet carpet.............$12.80   Grade F.................$12.85
Grade G..$14.20   Grade H...................................... 15.75

$175-$250

No. 2662 Bed Lounge. If you want something extra large and handsome, this will more than fill the bill. Frame is made of quarter-sawed oak, hand carved and highly polished. Has extra heavy legs, and body is richly carved. Length, 6 feet 4 inches; width, 48 inches. Has a woven wire bed with cotton top mattress. Back is extra high and very comfortable, and trimmed in silk plush to match base. Weight, 125 lbs.

Brussels carpet............$12.90   Velvet carpet.............$14.55   Grade F.................$14.50
Grade G ....$15.55   Grade H...................................... 16.75

$175-$250

Parlor and Wall Cabinets

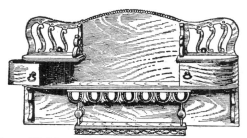

No. 145 Wall Cabinet. Made of imitation oak or mahogany finish, and highly polished. Size, 25x27 inches. Has two swinging side drawers and four shelves. Pretty and ornamental. Weight, 25 lbs.

Price, only..$2.25

$30-$40

No. 148 Wall Cabinet. This pretty little cabinet is made of quartered oak or mahogany finish, and polished. Size, 17x21 inches. Has fancy turned spindles and brass brackets at end of front railing. Has three shelves, and is a very good size. Weight, 15 lbs.

Price, only..$2.40

$30-$35

No. 144 Wall Cabinet. Made of whitewood, and beautifully finished in white enamel and gold, with brass brackets on top shelf. Size, 21x25 inches. Water rubbed and highly polished. A perfect beauty, and price exceedingly low. Weight, 20 lbs.

Price, only...$3.40

$30-$60

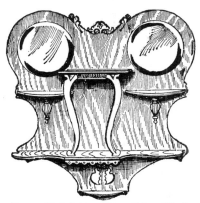

No. 135 Wall Cabinet. Beautifully polished, and made of quartered-oak or mahogany finish. Size, 24x24 inches. Has four shelves and two French bevel mirrors, 8 inches in diameter. An ornament to any parlor or sitting-room. Weight, 25 lbs.

Price, only $3.75

No. 134 Wall Cabinet. A very artistic and pretty design. Made of quartered-oak or mahogany finish, nicely carved and beautifully polished. Size, 22x24 inches. Has fine shelves and a fine 8x8 French bevel mirror. Weight, 15 lbs.

Price, only $2.40

$40-$65

Parlor and Wall Cabinets

No. 140 Wall Cabinet. Made of quartered oak or mahogany finish, carved and highly polished. Size, 23x24 inches. Has four shelves and a fancy finish bevel mirror, 8x10 inches. Weight, 27 lbs. Price, only....................................$2.95

$40-$60

No. 133 Wall Cabinet. Size, 25x22 inches. Has four shelves and an oval 6x10 French bevel mirror. Made of quartered-oak or mahogany finish. Has fancy turned spindles, and is highly hand polished. Weight, 20 lbs. Price, only....................................$2.70

$40-$60

No. 718 Parlor Cabinet. Made of oak or in mahogany finish. Height, 41 inches; width, 20 inches. Has a large shelf on top and two smaller below. All spindles are nicely turned and finished. A good size and pretty design. Weight, 40 lbs. Price, only....................................$3.25

$75-$100

No. 730 Parlor Cabinet. Artistic and refined design. Made of quarter-sawed oak or finished mahogany, and highly polished. Height, 46 inches; width, 24 inches. Has an 8x10 French bevel mirror in top, three small shelves, and a glass cabinet with door. A handsome odd piece for the parlor. Weight, 65 lbs. Price, only....................................$5.95

$115-$130

Parlor and Wall Cabinets

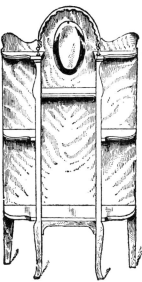

No. 731 Parlor Cabinet. Quartered-oak or mahogany finish, highly polished. Height, 46 inches; width, 23 inches. Has six shelves and a 6x10 French bevel mirror. Weight, 50 lbs.
Price, only $6.30

$75-$100

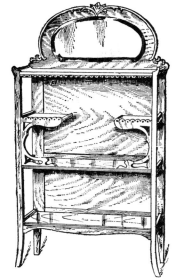

No. 728 Parlor Cabinet. Is beautifully polished and made of quartered oak or mahogany finished. Height, 55 inches; width, 29 inches. Has five shelves and a large 10x20 French bevel mirror. A very good size and ornamental design. Weight, 65 lbs.
Price, only $10.10

$75-$100

No. 725 Parlor Cabinet. If you want something extra fine and made of beautiful stock, this will please you. Quartered-oak or solid mahogany, hand carved and highly polished. Height, 61 inches; width, 32 inches. Has a large 12x22 French bevel mirror and seven shelves. Weight, 105 lbs.
Price, only.................................$19.20

$75-$100

No. 726 Parlor Cabinet. Made of solid mahogany or quartered-oak, hand carved and highly polished. Height, 57 inches; width, 32 inches. Has a French bevel mirror, 8x8, and one 10x18. The stock in this cabinet is extra select. Can be returned at our expense if not satisfactory. Weight, 118 lbs.
Price, only $17.85

$115-$130

Parlor and Wall Cabinets

No. 303 Corner Parlor Cabinet. Very orna
mental and nothing prettier. Made for the corner.
Height, 65 inches; width, 23 inches. Made of quartered oak or mahogany veneer. Hand carved and highly
polished. Has a glass door and French legs. Weight,
100 lbs.
Price, only.............................. .....$10.50

$75-$100

No. 727 Parlor Cabinet. This beautiful cabinet
is made of quartered-oak or solid mahogany, hand
carved and polished. Height, 56 inches; width, 31
inches. Has five shelves and fancy 16x16 French
bevel mirror. A plain but handsome design. Weight,
112 lbs.
Price, only $15.10

$50-$75

Iron Beds

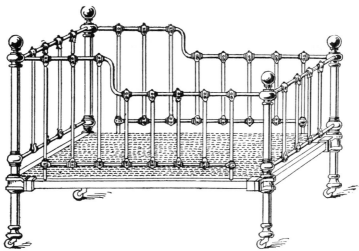

No. 1050 Child's Iron Crib. Made entirely of iron. Nicely ornamented with brass knobs and beautifully finished in the best white enamel. Made with and without drop sides, at same price. Be sure and state in your order which is desired. Weight, 50 pounds. Always clean and very ornamental. Price includes a fine woven wire spring with iron frame.

Size 2½x4½ ft. only..$6.75

$100-$150

This Bed

is only **$2.40**

in size 3x6½ feet.

No. 0116 Iron Bed. Very ornamental and pretty. Size of posts, 1 inch thick; other rails, ⅜ inch. Height at foot 39 inches; at head, 45 inches. Ornamented with brass knobs. Finished in three coats of the best white enamel. Well made and good value, and will surely please. Will give perfect satisfaction. Weight, 100 lbs.

Size 3 x6½ ft $2.40	Size 4 x6½ ft $3.20
Size 3½x6½ ft..................2.80	Size 4½x6½ ft...................3.65

$70-$90

Iron Beds

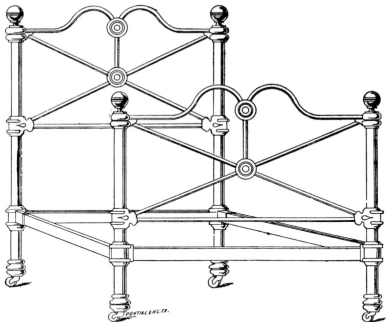

No. 0104 Iron Bed. We know this to be the best low priced bed on the market. Is strong and made of heavy tubing. Size of posts, 1 inch thick; other rails, ⅜ inch. Height at foot, 34 inches; at head, 40 inches. Ornamented with brass knobs. Finished in three coats of the best white enamel. Well made and good value. Will give perfect satisfaction. Weight, 100 pounds.
Size 3x6½ ft.......$3.25   Size 4x6½ ft........$3.25   Size 4½x6½ ft.....$3.25

$50-$75

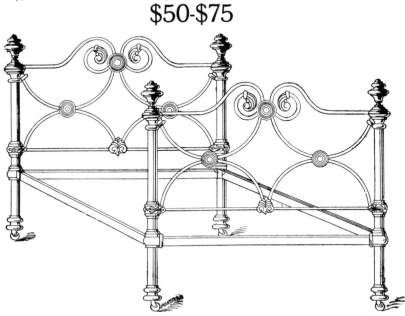

No. 0101 Iron Bed. This is a very ornamental design, and a great deal of work on it, considering the low price. It is well made, and posts are 1 inch thick and ornamented with brass knobs; also three brass rosettes in foot end and one in the head, which add to its beauty. Is just the right height and size to be pretty. Finished in white enamel. Weight, 100 pounds.
Size 3½x6½ ft .....$4.55   Size 4x6½ ft.......$4.55   Size 4½x6½ ft.....$4.55

$70-$90

Iron Beds

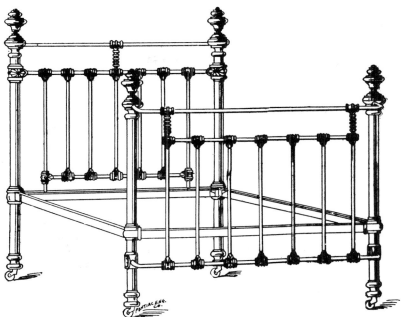

No. 0103 Iron Bed. This is a beauty for the money. Size of pillars, 1 inch; knobs, 2 inches; top rails, ⅝ inch; other rails, ⅜ inch. Height at foot, 38 inches; at head, 47 inches. Knobs are brass, and the bed is made with a swell or bow foot end, which gives it a very rich appearance. You make no mistake in ordering this, as we guarantee satisfaction. Finished in white enamel, and ball bearing casters. Weight, 100 pounds.
Size 3½ x 6½ ft......$4.90   Size 4x6½ ft.......$4.90   Size 4½ x6½ ft......$4.90

$75-$100

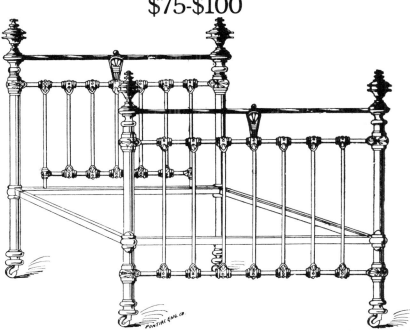

No. 9130 Iron Bed. This is extra good value. Has brass top rods and knobs. Richly finished in white enamel. Posts are 1 inch thick, and has the extended foot rail. Very neat, durable and cheap. Weight, 100 pounds. We have contracted for a large quantity of this style, otherwise we could not possibly make such a low price.
Size 3½x6½ ft.....$5.55   Size 4x6½ ft.......$5.55   Size 4½ x6½ ft.....$5.55

$100-$130

Iron Beds

No. 0108 Iron Bed. This is one of the most ornamental beds on the market. Is made with heavy fancy tubing, and posts are 1 inch thick. Is richly ornamented with brass top rods and knobs. Finished in the very finest white enamel. We are sure this will please you. The design is entirely new and very artistic. Weight, 100 lbs.

Size 4x6½ feet.............................$6.75   Size 4½x6½ feet.............................$6.75

$100-$150

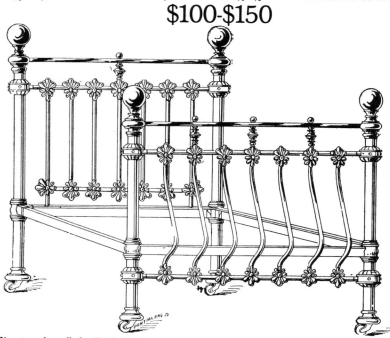

No. 4129 Iron Bed. Sleigh design. Very ornamental. Size of posts, 1 inch; knobs, 2 inches; top rails, ⅝ inch; other rails, ⅜ inch. Height at foot, 41 inches; at head, 55 inches. The bed is made with extended foot end, which adds to its richness. Fitted with ball bearing casters, and finished in white enamel. Top rods, knobs and spindles are brass. Weight, 100 lbs.

Size 4½x6½ feet.. .$6.95

$125-$160

Iron Beds

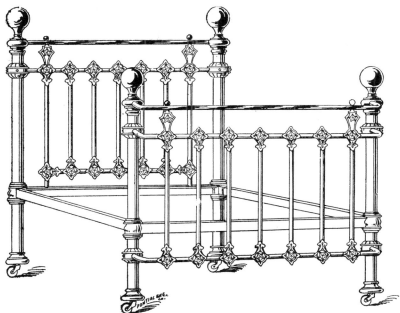

No. 1301 Iron Bed. This is also a very pretty design at a low price. Size of posts, 1 inch; knobs, 2 inches; top rails, ⅝ inch; other rails, ⅜ inch. Height at foot, 41 inches; at head, 55 inches. The bed is made with swell or bow extended foot end, which adds to its richness. Fitted with ball-bearing casters, and finished in white enamel. Top knobs and rods are brass. Weight, 100 lbs.
Size 4½x6½ feet, only.................. ....$6.90

$100-$150

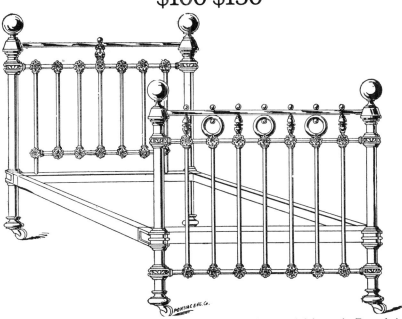

No. 4706 Iron Bed. Here is a beauty for the money. Has the extended foot end. Top rods, knobs, rings and small spindles are of brass. Size of posts, 1 inch; knobs, 2 inches; top rails, ⅝ inch; other rails, ⅜ inch. Height at head, 55 inches. Finished in white enamel, and ball bearing casters. This is one of our best sellers and a bargain.
Size 3½x6½ feet...........$7.50   Size 4x6½ feet...........$7.50   Size 4½x6½ feet...........$7.50
   No. 4706½. Same as above, except has swell or bow foot end, only $8.10.

$100-$150

Iron Beds

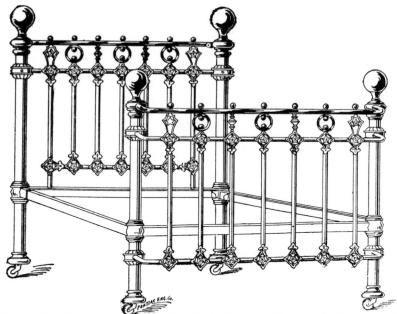

No. 1307 Iron Bed. One of our best styles. Made with extended foot end. Richly ornamented with brass top rods, knobs, spindles and rings. Size of posts, 1 inch; top rails, ⅝ inch; knobs, 2 inches; other rails, ⅜ inch. Height at foot, 41 inches; at head, 55 inches. Has ball-bearing casters, and finished in white enamel. Good value. Weight, 100 lbs.

Size 3½x6½ feet..... ......$8.75   Size 4x6½ feet............$8.75   Size 4½x6½ feet...........$8.75
4306, same as 1807, except is made without the swell foot end, only.....................................8.10

$100-$150

No. 4603 Iron Bed. Very artistic and handsome design. Is made with extended foot end, and posts are 1 inch thick. Is richly ornamented with brass top rods and knobs, and 14 brass rosettes in head and foot end. Finished in the very finest white enamel. We are sure this will please you. The design is entirely new and very ornamental.

Size 4x6½ feet...........................$10.50   Size 4½x6½ feet..............................$10.50

$125-$175

Brass Beds

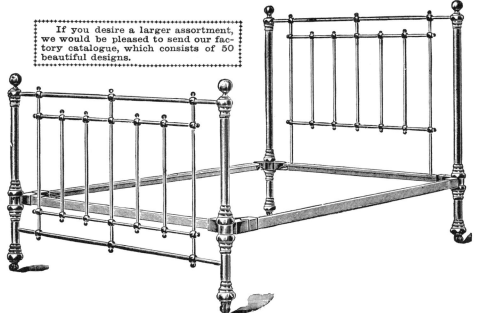

No. 202 Brass Bed. Spun brass knobs and mounts, and special ball bearings casters. Pillars, 1¼ inches; knobs, 2¼ inches; top rails, ⅝-inch; other rails, ½-inch. Height to top rail at head, 50 inches; at foot, 35 inches. Weight, 155 lbs. A great bargain at our price.

Size, 3½x6½ feet, only ....$23.50   Size, 4½x6½ feet................$23.50

$200-$250

No. 657 Brass Bed. The cheapest swell-foot on the market. A beautiful, rich and very popular design. Spun brass knobs and mounts. Pillars, 1¼ inches; knobs, 2¼ inches; top rails, ⅝-inch; other rails, ½-inch. Height to top rail at foot, 37 inches; at head, 55 inches. This will more than please you. Satisfaction guaranteed. Weight, 175 lbs.

Size, 4½x6½ feet, only $29.75

$250-$350

Brass Beds

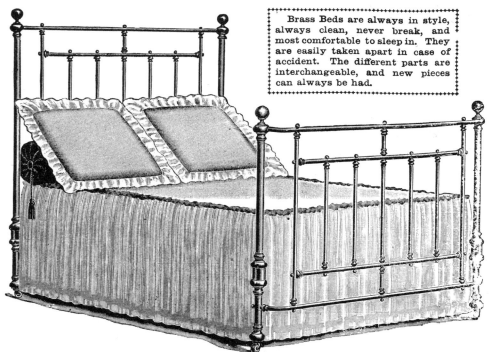

Brass Beds are always in style, always clean, never break, and most comfortable to sleep in. They are easily taken apart in case of accident. The different parts are interchangeable, and new pieces can always be had.

No. 203 Brass Bed. Very pretty and rich design. Made with extended bow or swell-foot end. Spun brass knobs and mounts, ball bearing casters. Pillars, 1¼ inches; knobs, 2¼ inches; top rails, ⅝-inch; other rails, ½-inch. Height to top rail at head, 55 inches; at foot, 37 inches. Weight, 160 lbs.
Size, 3½x6½ feet, without drapery..$26.60   Size, 4½x6½ feet, without drapery..$26.60

$275-$350

No. 664 Brass Bed. Spun brass knobs and mounts, and ball bearing casters. Pillars, 1½ inches; knobs, 2¾ inches; top rails, ¾-inch; other rails, ⅝-inch. Height to top rail at head, 62 inches; at foot, 37 inches. Made with swell-foot end. A good, heavy bed for little money. Weight, 175 lbs.
Size, 3½x6½ feet, only...........$32.90   Size, 4½x6½ feet, only $32.90

$300-$375

Brass Beds

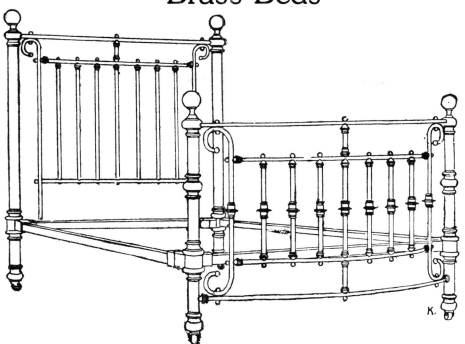

No. 670 Brass Bed. Heavy and large design. Has spun brass mounts and knobs. Pillars, 1½ inches; knobs, 2¾ inches; top rails, ¾-inch; other rails, ⅝-inch. Height to top rail at foot, 37 inches; at head, 55 inches. Made with swell-foot end. Weight, 175 lbs. Extra good value.
Size, 4½ x 6½ feet, only $36.40

$275-$375

No. 650 Brass Bed. The best and prettiest style on the market for the money. Size of pillars, 2 inches; knobs, 3½ inches; top rails, ¾-inch; other rails, ⅝-inch. Height to top rail at foot, 37 inches; at head, 55 inches. Weight 175 lbs. This is a special bargain at our price. Has the swell (bow) foot end.
Size, 4½ x 6½ feet, only $49.00

$375-$500

Mantel and Upright Folding Beds

No. 9 Cabinet Mantel Bed. Well made of elm and nicely finished. Has a good, large 18x40 inch German bevel mirror and a fine woven wire supported spring and mattress clamps. Width, 4 feet 2 inches. Very ornamental, and price is low. Weight, 275 lbs.
Price complete, only...$18.60

$175-$215

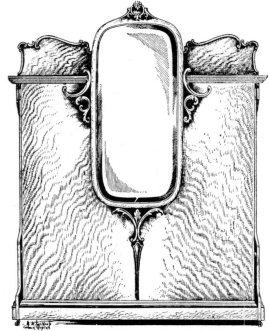

No. 25 Cabinet Mantel Bed. Made of the very finest quarter-sawed oak richly hand carved and highly hand polished. Width of bed when open, 4 feet 2 inches. Fitted with a fine woven wire supported spring. Has a beautiful 18x40 inch oval French bevel mirror. Is exceedingly ornamental and a very artistic design. Weight, 275 lbs.
Price, only..$24.30

$190-$230

No. 500 Upright Folding Bed. Well made of solid oak, richly carved. Size, when open, 4 feet 4 inches wide, 6 feet 2 inches long. Has a good 18x40 inch German bevel mirror; also fitted with fine woven wire supported spring and mattress clamps. Has the automatic lock, which makes it perfectly safe. A fine bed for little money. Weight, 375 lbs.
Price complete, only...$18.75

$175-$215

No. 501 Upright Folding Bed. Well made of oak, with quarter-sawed panels, richly carved and highly hand polished. Size of bed when open, 4 ft. 4 in. wide, 6 ft. 2 in. long. Has a fine woven wire supported spring and a large 18x40 inch pattern plate French bevel mirror. Has mattress clamps and an automatic lock. Good design, and will guarantee satisfaction. Weight, 400 lbs. Price complete, only.....................$26.95

$175-$215

Combination Folding Beds

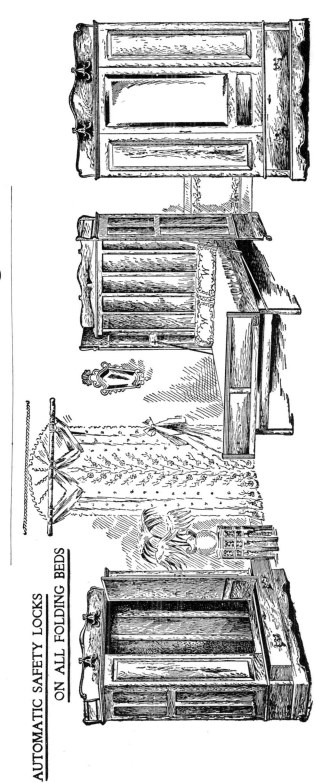

$150-$175

$200-$215

$250-$275

No. 69 Combination Folding Bed and Wardrobe. Carved and nicely finished. Size of bed when open, 4 feet wide, 6 feet 3 inches long. Has a good 18x40 inch German bevel mirror door, very large wardrobe space, which is nicely fitted with hooks. The bed folds up in the back. For method of operating same, see description below. The bed has a fine woven wire mattress. Weight, about 400 lbs. Extra good value and cheap. Price, in elm, without mirror, $20.00; in elm, with mirror, $25.00; in solid oak, with mirror, $27.50.

Combination Folding Beds

$210-$240

$180-$225

No. 83 Combination Folding Bed, Writing Desk, Bookcase and Wardrobe. Made in elm, with oak panels, neatly carved and finished antique. Has a good 18 x 20 inch German bevel mirror. Size of bed, 4 feet wide, 6 feet 3 inches long. Has a good woven wire mattress. Weight, 400 lbs. For method of operating above bed, see description below. Desk is nicely partitioned with pigeon holes, and wardrobe is fitted with hooks. The best bed on the market for the money. Price, complete, only $22.95.

Combination Folding Beds

$275-$325

$175-$190

$375-$425

No. 80 Combination Wardrobe, Writing Desk, Bookcase and Folding Bed. Made of elm or oak. Richly hand carved and nicely finished. Has a fine, large 18 x 40 inch German bevel mirror. The wardrobe part contains hooks, and the writing desk is partitioned with pigeon hole and drawer. Has one large and two small drawers under desk. For method of operating above bed, see description below. Size of bed when open, 4 feet wide, 6 feet 3 inches long. Has a fine woven wire spring in the bed, and also contains an automatic lock. Weight, 450 lbs. Price, in elm, only $27.95; in oak, only $33.25.

METHOD OF OPERATING ABOVE FOLDING BEDS; The beds lower from the back instead of the front. By this method better ventilation is secured, and the front is left undisturbed. While the above beds occupy no more floor space than any other, they contain from three to six other pieces of furniture besides a comfortable bed. The bedding and pillows can be arranged ready for occupancy, and assured of good ventilation, and be lowered ready for use in a moment by simply swinging one end from the wall. We use a 3-inch lignum-vitæ wheel caster, which cannot wear carpets, and renders the bed very easy to move. The legs have an automatic movement which makes it impossible for them to close while bed is occupied. Directions on each bed.

53

Combination Folding Beds

MADE BY THE FINEST OF CABINET MAKERS AND FINISHERS

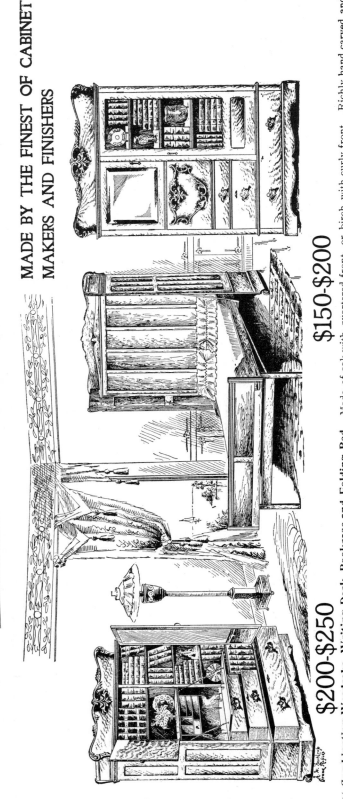

$150-$200

$375-$415

$200-$250

No. 64½ Combination Wardrobe, Writing Desk, Bookcase and Folding Bed. Made of oak with quartered front, or birch with curly front. Richly hand carved and highly polished. Has a fine, large 18x20 inch French bevel mirror. The wardrobe part contains hooks, and the writing desk is partitioned with pigeon holes and drawers. Has one large and two small drawers under desk. (For method of operating above bed, see page 28.) Size of bed when open, 4 feet wide, 6 feet 3 inches long. Has a fine woven wire spring in the bed, and also contains an automatic lock. Weight, 450 pounds. Price in oak or birch, only..$37.75

54

Combination Folding Beds

$200-$275

$300-$350

$160-$200

No. 64 **Combination Folding Bed, Wardrobe, Writing Desk and Bookcase.** Well made of quarter-sawed oak or birch, nicely hand carved. Has a good, large 18x40 inch French bevel mirror and is nicely partitioned with pigeon holes and drawers, and wardrobe is fitted with hooks. Bed lets down from back. Size of bed when open, 4 feet wide, 6 feet 3 inches long. Has a fine woven wire spring. For method of operating above bed, see page 28. Weight, about 400 pounds. Price complete, only $39.00

Combination Folding Beds

$300-$350

$200-$250

No. 82 Combination Folding Bed, Bookcase and Writing Desk. Made of solid oak with quartered front, or curly birch, richly hand carved and polished like a piano. Has large 12x22 and 14x50 inch French bevel mirrors above desk. All shelves are adjustable. Desk is nicely partitioned with pigeon holes and drawer. Has four drawers under desk made with swell front. Size of bed, 4 feet wide, 6 feet 3 inches long. Has the automatic safety lock, and a fine woven wire spring. For method of operating this bed, see page 28. Weight, about 400 pounds. The stock in this bed is very select and beautiful. Price complete, only.................................$53.00

New Safety Draw Beds

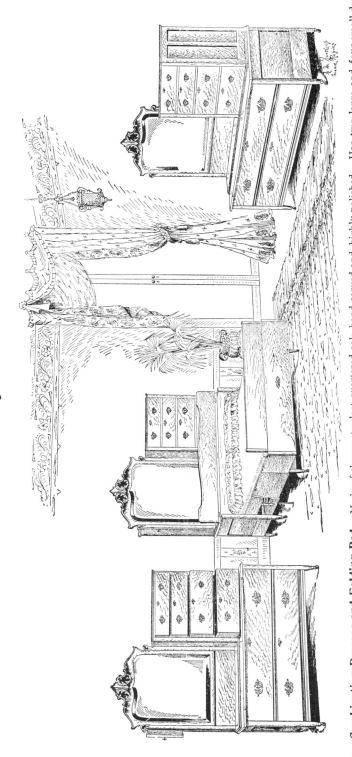

$300-$375

No. 73. Combination Dresser and Folding Bed. Made of the most select quartered oak, hand carved and highly polished. Has two large and four small drawers, with locks, and a large 24x30 inch pattern French bevel mirror; also a large place for hats on left side, where door opens. Bed pulls out from lower part, as cut shows it. Bed is fitted with a fine woven wire supported spring. Makes a very handsome dresser, and a very cheap piece of furniture, considering the two pieces. Size of bed when open, 4 feet 2 inches wide, 6 feet 2 inches long. Directions on each bed. Weight, 300 pounds. Price, in oak. $39.95

New Safety Draw Beds

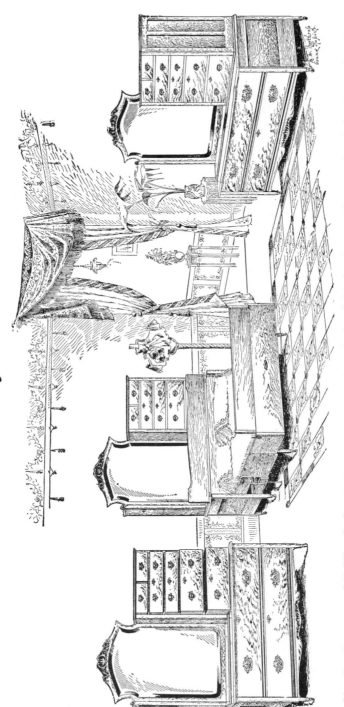

$300-$400

No. 71. Combination Dresser and Folding Bed. Similar to No. 73, except is much nicer finished and made of better stock. Bed pulls out from lower part, and as you close it, it folds twice and pushes up in back of case. Has two large and six small drawers. Size of bed when open, 4 feet 2 inches wide, 6 feet 2 inches long. Has a good woven wire supported spring. Also an extra large, fine 29x40 inch pattern French bevel mirror, very useful and ornamental. Has a door on left side for hats. Handles are made of cast brass. Weight, 300 pounds. Read note at top of page. Price, in oak............$46.80 Price, in curly birch............$49.50

New Safety Draw Beds

$450-$500

No. 72 Combination Bookcase, Writing Desk and Folding Bed. Has two large drawers and a cupboard in lower part. The desk on right side is nicely partitioned with pigeon holes and drawer. The bookcase has two glass doors, and all shelves are adjustable. Has a very pretty 16x20 inch oval French bevel mirror. Bed pulls out from lower part, and as you close it, it folds twice and pushes up in back of case. Size of bed when open, 4 feet 2 inches wide, 6 feet 2 inches long. Also has a good woven wire spring. This piece is very cheap, as you are getting three pieces of furniture at the price of one good bed. Weight, 300 pounds. Price, in curly birch . . . . . $52.00 Price, in quartered oak $49.40

Chamber Suits

Bed to Nos. 140 and 140½ Suits. Made of select oak, richly hand carved and highly polished. Bed has raised panel. Height, 6 feet; slat, 4 feet 6 inches. Suits Nos. 140 and 140½ consists of bed, dresser and commode. Has heavy posts. Well made and cheap. There is nothing on the market to compare with this at our price.

$90-$115

No. 140½ Cheval Suit. Made of oak, carved and polished. Size of dresser top, 20x60 inches. Has a good, large 18x40 inch German bevel mirror. Suit is made of heavy stock and highly finished. Has two large and two small drawers, and a hat cabinet. Weight, 300 lbs.
Price, complete, only $17.95

$150-$175

No. 140 Suit. Made of select oak, carved and highly polished. Dresser has a good, large 24x30 inch German bevel mirror, and is made with double top. The polish and cabinet work on this suit is extra fine. Has two large and two small drawers. Weight, 300 lbs.
Price, complete, only $15.95

$100-$125

Chamber Suits

Bed to Nos. 141 and 141½ Suits. Made of good oak, richly hand carved and highly polished. Has raised panel, richly finished. Height, 6 feet; slat, 4 feet 6 inches. Suit consists of bed, dresser and commode. A bargain at our price. Extra large and very ornamental.

$90-$115

No. 141 Suit. Made of select oak, beautifully carved, and polished like a piano. Dresser is made with double top, and has a good, large 24x30 inch German bevel mirror. The carving on this suit is very showy and rich. Weight, 300 lbs.
Our bargain price is only..$17.95

$120-$140

No. 141½ Cheval Suit. Made of select oak, carved and highly polished. Has double top and a large 18x40 inch German bevel mirror. A very convenient style, especially for ladies. This is extra well made and worth double our price. Weight, 300 lbs. A suit that is hard to beat. Price, only...$18.95

$150-$175

Chamber Suits

$125-$150 $125-$150 $95-$110

No. 143 Chamber Suit. Made of select oak, richly hand carved and highly polished. Height of bed, 6 feet 2 inches; slat, 4 feet 6 inches. Bed has a beautiful raised panel, and foot and head boards are richly carved. The dresser is very pretty, with French legs and heavy base, and has a good large 24x30 inch German bevel mirror. The dresser and commode are made with double tops. Extra heavy stock in this suit, and a style that will surely please you. Weight, 300 lbs. This is a bargain at only.............................$21.80

Chamber Suits

Bed to Nos. 144 and 144½ Suits. This is a beauty. Made of the finest oak, handsomely carved and highly polished. Has a raised panel, richly polished. Height, 6 feet 2 inches; slat, 4 feet 6 inches. The foot board is also carved. Suit consists of bed, dresser and commode.

$110-$150

No. 144½ Cheval Suit. This is a very pretty design with a great deal of work. Made of solid oak, beautifully hand carved and highly polished. Has a large 18x40 inch German bevel mirror and French legs. Has large drawers with locks and a hat cabinet. Weight, 300 lbs. Price, only $22.75

$150-$200

No. 144 Suit. Made of select oak. Has very heavy carving and highly polished; double top and French legs. The mirror is 24x30 inch, German bevel. A fine, large suit for little money. A rich design, and one that will please you.
Price, complete, only..$22.80

$125-$150

Chamber Suits

Bed to Nos. 146 and 146½ Suits. Made of select oak, richly carved and very highly polished. Height, 6 feet 2 inches; slat 4 feet 6 inches. Extra heavy and well made. Foot and head boards are handsomely carved and have raised panels. Suits consist of bed, dresser and commode.

$110-$150

No. 146 Suit. Made of oak, carved and highly polished. Dresser has a fine 24x30 inch fancy French bevel mirror and French legs, and top drawers are made with serpentine fronts. All handles are cast brass. Dresser and commode are made with double tops. Our price on this suit is very low, considering construction and finish. Weight, 300 lbs. Price, complete, only $23.95

$125-$150

No. 146½ Cheval Suit. Made of select oak, beautifully carved and highly polished. Dresser has French legs, locks to drawers, and an 18x40 fancy French bevel mirror. Handles are made of cast brass. Weight, 300 lbs. Good value, and will last forever.
Price, complete, only $24.95

$150-$200

Chamber Suits

Bed to Nos. 145 and 145½ Suits. This is a beauty. Made of the finest oak, handsomely carved and highly polished. Has two raised panels, richly polished. Height, 6 feet 2 inches; slat, 4 feet 6 inches. The foot board is also carved. Note the great amount of carving on this suit, is all hand work. The suit generally sells for double our price. Suit consists of bed, dresser and commode.

$110-$150

No. 145 Suit. Made of select oak. Has very heavy carving and highly polished; double top and French legs. The mirror is 24x30 inch, a fancy French bevel plate, and the top drawers are made with serpentine fronts. Has extra heavy base. A fine, large suit for little money. A rich design, and one that will more than please you.
Price, complete...$24.95

No. 145½ Cheval Suit. This is a very pretty design with a great deal of work. Made of solid oak, beautifully hand carved and highly polished. Has a large 18x40 fancy French bevel mirror and French legs. Has large drawers with locks and a hat cabinet. This is a massive and rich design. Base is extra heavy. Weight, 300 lbs.
Price, only $25.95

$125-$150

$150-$200

Chamber Suits

$80-$100

$130-$160

$115-$150

No. 148 Chamber Suit. This is a little beauty, and an ornament to any bedroom. Made of select oak, with raised panels, handsomely hand carved and highly polished. Dresser has a beautiful, large 24x30 inch pattern plate French bevel mirror. Has French legs and double tops, and extra heavy base. The top drawers are made with shaped serpentine fronts and fitted with the finest of cast brass handles. Head and foot boards of bed are richly hand carved. Height, 6 feet 2 inches; slat, 4 feet 6 inches. A very heavy and well made suit for little money. Weight, 300 pounds. Our price on this suit is very low, considering finish and construction. Price, complete............................ $25.80

66

Chamber Suits

$150-$200 $110-$150 $80-$100

No. 147 Chamber Suit. Made of select oak, richly hand carved and highly hand polished. Height of bed, 6 feet 2 inches; slat, 4 feet 6 inches. Bed has two beautiful raised panels, and foot and head boards are richly carved. The dresser is very pretty, with French legs, and has an extra large 28x34 fancy French bevel mirror. The dresser and commode are made with double tops, and the top drawers of dresser are made with shaped serpentine fronts, and fitted with the finest of cast brass handles. Extra heavy stock in this suit, and a style that will surely please you. Weight, 300 pounds. This is a bargain at only................................$27.80

Chamber Suits

$115-$150

$120-$150

$75-$100

No. 153 Chamber Suit. This large, heavy suit is made of quartered oak, beautifully hand carved, rubbed and highly polished. Bed has raised panels and richly carved. Slat is 4 feet 6 inches. Dresser has an extra large 28x34 inch French bevel mirror, two large and two small drawers, and the finest of cast brass handles. Suit consists of bed, dresser and commode. Has double top and French legs. Weight, 300 pounds. Price, complete, only..................$30.75

(Wrong cut. The commode to this suit is the same as in No. 147 Suit.

Chamber Suits

Bed to Nos. 408 and 407 Suits. Made of quarter-sawed oak, carved and highly polished. Height, 6 feet 4 inches; slat, 4 feet 6 inches; length, 6 feet 2 inches. Foot of bed is neatly carved. Suit consists of bed, dresser and commode.

$150-$200

No. 407 Suit. Made of quarter-sawed oak, richly carved and highly polished. Size of top, 24x48 inches. Made with swell front. Has a large 30x40 inch French bevel mirror. Height, 6 feet 6 inches. Weight, 300 pounds. Very large and massive.
Price complete, only..$35.75

$200-$250

No. 408 Suit. Made of quarter-sawed oak, carved and highly polished. Dresser has an extra large 30x36 inch French bevel mirror, two large and two small drawers, with locks. Very solid and well made. Size of top, 24x48 inches. Height, 6 feet 6 inches.
Price complete, only..$35.65

$150-$200

69

Chamber Suits

Bed to Nos. 413 and 415 Suits. All beautifully hand carved and polished like a mirror. Made of quarter-sawed oak. Height, 6 feet 4 inches: slat, 4 feet 6 inches; length, 6 feet 2 inches. A massive design, and one that will please you. Suit consists of bed, dresser and commode.

$175-$225

No. 413 Cheval Chamber Suit. Made of quarter-sawed oak, carved and highly polished. Size of top, 24x48 inches. Has shaped top and swell top drawer. All drawers have locks, and handles are made of cast brass. Height, 6 feet 8 inches. Has a fine, large 20x40 inch French bevel plate mirror. A handsome suit for little money. Weight, 300 pounds. Price complete, only.................................$39.95

$175-$200

No. 415 Cheval Chamber Suit. Made of oak, handsomely carved and highly polished. Has double shaped top. Locks to all drawers and cast brass handles. Has a large 30x40 inch pattern French plate mirror. Weight, 350 pounds. Size of top, 24x54 inches. Height, 6 feet 8 inches. Price complete, only.................................$46.55

$200-$260

Chamber Suits

$110-$135

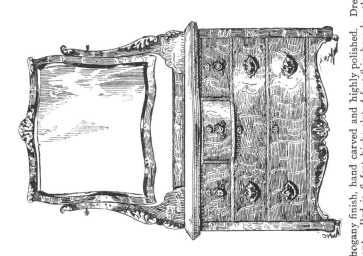

$115-$150

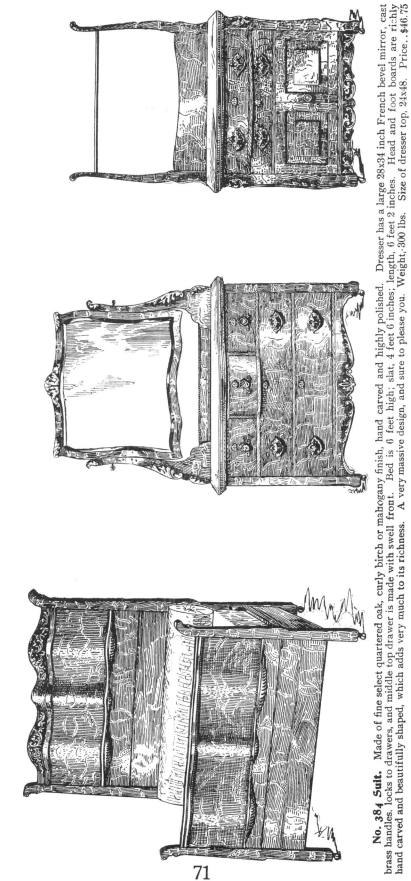

$115-$135

No. 384 Suit. Made of fine select quartered oak, curly birch or mahogany finish, hand carved and highly polished. Dresser has a large 28x34 inch French bevel mirror, cast brass handles, locks to drawers, and middle top drawer is made with swell front. Bed is 6 feet high; slat, 4 feet 6 inches; length, 6 feet 2 inches. Head and foot boards are richly hand carved and beautifully shaped, which adds very much to its richness. A very massive design, and sure to please you. Weight, 300 lbs. Size of dresser top, 24x48. Price..$46.75

Chamber Suits

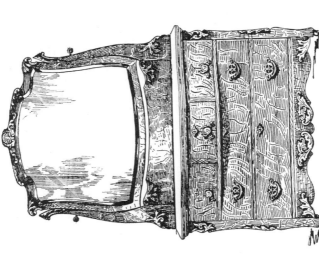

$120-$145

$125-$150

$115-$135

No. 381 Suit. Made of quartered oak, curly birch or mahogany finish, hand carved and highly polished. Dresser has a large 30x36 inch French bevel mirror, cast brass handles, locks to drawers, and top drawers are made with swell front. Bed is 6 feet; slat, 4 feet 6 inches; length, 6 feet 2 inches. Head and foot boards are richly hand carved, beautifully shaped, which adds very much to its richness. A very massive and artistic design. Weight, 300 lbs. Size of dresser top, 24x48 inches. Price, complete.........$53.20

Chamber Suits

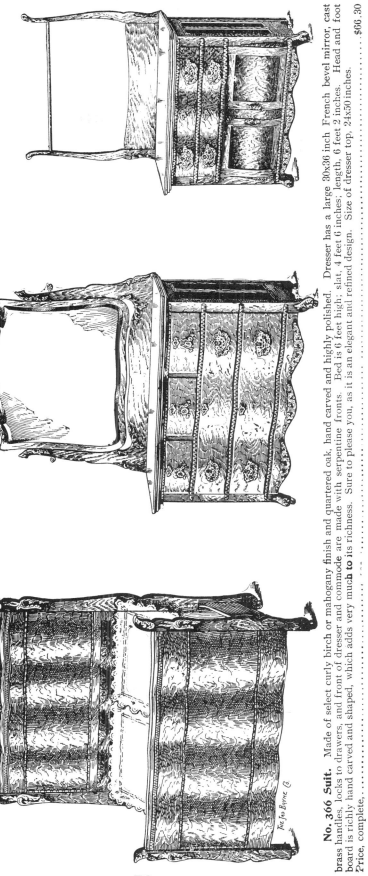

$100-$125

$140-$175

$125-$150

No. 366 Suit. Made of select curly birch or mahogany finish and quartered oak, hand carved and highly polished. Dresser has a large 30x36 inch French bevel mirror, cast brass handles, locks to drawers, and front of dresser and commode are made with serpentine fronts. Bed is 6 feet high; slat, 4 feet 6 inches; length, 6 feet 2 inches. Head and foot board is richly hand carved and shaped, which adds very much to its richness. Sure to please you, as it is an elegant and refined design. Size of dresser top, 24x50 inches. Price, complete, ... $66.30

Chamber Suits

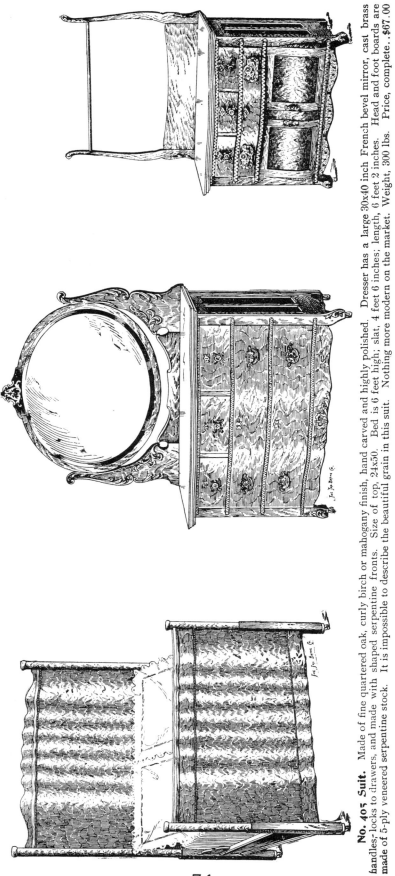

$100-$130

$140-$175

$90-$120

No. 405 Suit. Made of fine quartered oak, curly birch or mahogany finish, hand carved and highly polished. Dresser has a large 30x40 inch French bevel mirror, cast brass handles; locks to drawers, and made with shaped serpentine fronts. Size of top, 24x50. Bed is 6 feet high; slat, 4 feet 6 inches; length, 6 feet 2 inches. Head and foot boards are made of 5-ply veneered serpentine stock. It is impossible to describe the beautiful grain in this suit. Nothing more modern on the market. Weight, 300 lbs. Price, complete..$67.00

Odd Dressers

No. 22 Dresser. Well made of solid oak, carved and highly polished. A beauty for the money. Top, 20x46 inches. Has a beautiful, large 24x30 inch German bevel mirror. Well made and a bargain. One of the latest design on the market. Weight, 150 lbs. Price, only $9.35

$90-$120

No. 23 Dresser. Made of select oak, carved and highly polished. Has a fine, large 24x30 inch French bevel mirror. Base is extra heavy and has two large and two small drawers. Top, 21x46 inches. Shaped top and cast brass handles. Weight, 150 lbs. Price, only $10.95

$110-$160

No. 24 Dresser. New design, with extra heavy base. Made of select oak, carved and highly polished. Has a fine, large 24x30 inch French bevel mirror. Top, 21x46 inches. Shaped top and cast brass handles. Weight, 150 lbs. Very artistic and ornamental. Price, only $11.35

$110-$160

No. 27 Dresser. Richly carved and highly polished. Has a very handsome 24x30 inch French bevel mirror. Top, 21x46 inches. Has two large and two small drawers. Shaped top, and two top drawers are made with serpentine front; cast brass handles. Price, solid oak, only $12.90

$120-$170

Odd Dressers

No. 522 Dresser. Top, 21x44 inches. Richly hand carved and polished like a mirror. Has extra large mirror, size 24x30 inches, French bevel. Cast brass handles and locks to drawers and top drawers have swell front. Weight, 150 lbs.
Price, oak or mahogany finish....................................$14.25
Enameled white.. 15.50

$95-$150

No. 519 Dresser. Size of top, 21x44 inches. Hand carved and highly polished. Has a fine, large 24x30 inch French bevel mirror. Locks to all drawers and cast brass handles. Top drawers made with swell front. Weight, 150 lbs. A beauty.
Price, in oak or mahogany finish...........................$13.90
Enameled white... 15.40

$90-$120

No. 521 Dresser. Exceedingly ornamental. Top, 21x44 inches. Has a good, large 24x30 inch French bevel mirror. All drawers have locks and swell fronts to top drawers. Hand carved and highly polished. Weight, 150 lbs.
Price, oak or mahogany finish..........................$13.30
Enameled white.. 14.30

$100-$150

Odd Dressers

No. 524 Dresser. Beautifully carved and polished. Top, 21x44 inches, made of birdseye maple or mahogany finish. Has a fine, large 24x30 inch French bevel mirror. Has shaped top and cast brass handles. All drawers have locks, and richly shaped. Very ornamental and cheap.
Price...$24.50
Enameled white.. 24.62

$75-$110

No. 525 Dresser. Made of select birdseye maple. Richly carved and highly polished. Has a very handsome 24x30 inch French bevel mirror. Top, 21x46 inches. Has two large and two small drawers. Shaped top with serpentine front and cast brass handles.
Price...$23.00
Enameled white........... .... 23.00

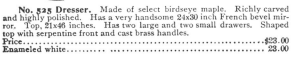

$75-$110

No. 526 Dresser. Top, 21x44 inches. Richly hand carved and polished like a mirror. Has extra large mirror, size 24x30 inches, French bevel. Cast brass handles and locks to drawers. Weight, 150 lbs. Made of select birdseye maple or mahogany finish, and serpentine front and French legs. Price..$22.25
Enameled white.. 22.25

$75-$110

Chiffoniers and Wardrobes

No. 612 Chiffonier. Well made of solid oak and highly polished, and top drawer has swell front. Very large and useful. Height, 4 feet 10 inches; width, 30 inches; depth, 18 inches. Has five large drawers with locks. Weight, 120 lbs. Extra value and a bargain. Our price is only.........................$8.60

$90-$115

No. 614 Chiffonier. A very ornamental and useful style. Made of solid oak and highly polished, with swell top drawer. Height, 6 feet 1 inch; size of top, 21x30 inches. Has a good 16x18 inch French bevel mirror, five large drawers with locks. Weight, 125 lbs. Price, only.........................$12.30

$115-$135

No. 615 Chiffonier. Made of select oak or mahogany finish, hand carved and highly polished; has a good, large 14x22 inch French bevel mirror and five large drawers. Size of top, 21x30 inches; top drawer has swell front. Weight, 125 lbs. Price.......$13.30

$115-$150

No. 618 Chiffonier. Made of select oak or mahogany finish, richly carved and highly polished. Size of top, 21x36 inches. Has a large 16x24 inch French bevel mirror. Has shaped top and cast brass handles, and top drawer is also nicely shaped. Weight, 135 lbs. Price.............................$13.95

$115-$150

Chiffoniers and Wardrobes

No. 613 Chiffonier. Well made of oak, hand carved and highly polished. Size of top, 21x30 inches. Has five large drawers. Also a fine, large 14x22 inch French bevel mirror. Has shaped top drawer and brass handles. Weight, 125 lbs. Oak or mahogany finish. Price, only $13.00

$115-$135

No. 616 Chiffonier. Made of select oak or mahogany finish, carved and highly polished. Size of top, 21x36 inches. Has five large drawers, with cast brass handles, and top drawer made with serpentine front. Very large, roomy and cheap. Locks to all drawers. Weight, 135 lbs. Price, in oak......$10.35

$90-$115

No. 623 Chiffonier. Well made of oak, hand carved and highly polished. Size of top, 21x36 inches. Has four large and two small drawers and a hat cabinet. Also a fine, large 14x26 inch French bevel mirror; has shaped double top and cast brass handles and shaped top drawer. Weight, 135 lbs. Oak or mahogany finish. Price, only.................$14.65

$125-$160

No. 630 Chiffonier. Made of bird's eye maple or mahogany finish. Size of top, 21x36 inches. Has five large drawers, all beautifully shaped and French legs. Also a large 16x24 inch French bevel mirror. Nothing handsomer made. Weight, 135 lbs. Price...................................$21.75

$115-$135

Chiffoniers and Wardrobes

No. 51 Wardrobe. Made of oak, carved and nicely finished. Very ornamental and pretty. Height, 7 feet 4 inches; width, 3 feet 1 inch. Has door and drawer. Also fitted with hooks. Weight, 100 lbs.
Price, in solid oak............................$10.40
Price, in curly birch........................ 14.85

$140-$180

No. 52 Wardrobe. Made of oak or birch, carved and richly finished. Height, 7 feet 4 inches; width, 3 feet 1 inch. Has a door with lock, and one drawer. Inside is fitted with hooks. Weight, 100 lbs. Has a large 18x40 inch French bevel mirror.
Price in solid oak............. ....$14.45
Price, in curly birch........................ 19.20

$200-$240

No. 56 Wardrobe. Made of fine oak, hand carved and highly hand polished. Height, 8 feet; width, 4 feet 3 inches. Very large and heavy. Inside is fitted with hooks. Two doors and two drawers.
Price.......................................$18.00
Price, with 14x48 inch French bevel mirrors in doors................................... 30.00

$225-$275

No. 55 Wardrobe. Made of oak and highly hand polished. Height, 7 feet 9 inches; width, 4 feet. Inside is fitted with hooks. Doors and drawers have locks. Very ornamental and fine enough for any one. Weight, 175 lbs. Price, only.................$16.80
Price, with 14x48 inch French bevel mirrors in doors................................... 28.70

$225-$275

Hall Trees

No. 428 Hall Tree. Made of quartered oak, hand carved and highly polished. Height, 77 inches; width, 36 inches; depth, 17 inches. Has a fine 12x12 inch French bevel mirror, four large hat hooks, an umbrella holder, and the seat is made with lid for rubbers. Very ornamental and a bargain at our price. Weight, 100 lbs. Our price, only............$10.90

$175-$215

No. 205 Hall Tree. Made of quarter-sawed oak. Height, 84 inches; width, 36 inches. Hand carved and highly hand polished. Has a large 16x24 inch French bevel mirror, four large double hat hooks and an umbrella holder. Seat is made with lid for rubbers. Weight, 100 lbs. Extra large rack for the money. Price, only............$14.10

$175-$200

No. 206 Hall Tree. Very large and a rich design. Made of quartered oak, hand carved and polished. Height, 6 feet 9 inches; width, 3 feet. Has a large 18x28 oval French bevel mirror, four large double hat hooks, an umbrella holder, and a lid to seat for rubbers. Has large, heavy arms. Rich and handsome. Weight, 150 lbs. Price............$16.95

$175-$200

No. 238 Hall Tree. Made of quartered oak, hand carved and highly polished. Has a very large mirror, size 18 x 40 inches, French bevel quality. Height, 6 feet 10 inches; width, 3 feet. Has an umbrella holder, four double hooks and a lid to seat. Weight, 150 lbs. Price, only............$16.10

$175-$200

Hall Trees

No. 315 Hall Tree. Very ornamental design. Made of quartered oak, hand carved and highly polished. Height, 78 inches; width, 38 inches. Has a good 16-inch circle French bevel mirror, four double hat hooks, an umbrella holder, and seat has a lid for rubbers. Weight, 100 lbs. Price, only.......$13.25

$200-$250

No. 342 Hall Tree. Made of quarter-sawed oak, hand carved and highly polished. Height, 6 feet 8 inches; width, 37 inches. Has a 16x26 inch German bevel mirror. Made with lid to seat for rubbers. Has four double hooks and an umbrella holder. Weight, 80 lbs. Price, only..........................$14.25

$200-$225

No. 307 Hall Tree. An artistic and refined design. Made of quartered oak, hand carved and highly polished. Has four double hat hooks, an umbrella holder, a lid to seat and a fine large 24x30 inch French bevel mirror. Height, 6 feet 8 inches; width, 4 feet. Rich and elegant. Weight, 100 lbs. Our bargain price is only.....................$17.85

$200-$225

No. 341 Hall Tree. Made of quartered oak, hand carved and highly hand polished. Height, 7 feet 1 inch; width, 3 feet 2 inches. Has a beautiful 20x36 inch French bevel mirror, four large double hat hooks, an umbrella holder and a lid to seat for rubbers. Extra heavy and large. Worth double our price. Weight, about 160 lbs. Price, only....$20.25

$175-$215

Hall Trees

No. 118 Hall Tree. Made of quartered oak, richly hand carved and highly polished. Height, 7 feet; width, 4 feet 6 inches. Has a beautiful large 34x38 inch French bevel mirror, four double hat hooks, a large lid to seat for rubbers. This rack is fine enough for any home. Very large and a handsome design. Weight, 175 lbs. Price....................$35.00

$250-$300

No. 319 Hall Tree. Rich and handsome. Made of quarter-sawed oak, hand carved and highly polished. Has four large double hat hooks, an umbrella holder and a lid to seat. Has a large, beautiful 18x26 inch French bevel mirror. Height, 6 feet; width, 3 feet 2 inches. Weight, 160 lbs. Price....................$19.50

$250-$300

No. 345 Hall Tree. Made of quartered oak, hand carved and highly hand polished. Height, 7 feet 2 inches; width, 3 feet 9 inches. Has a beautiful 24x30 inch French bevel mirror, four large double hat hooks, an umbrella holder and a lid to seat for rubbers. Extra heavy and large. Worth double our price. Weight, about 180 lbs. Price, only.......$23.90

$250-$300

Parlor Tables and Jardiniere Stands

 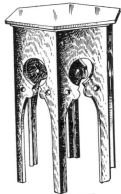

No. 302 Tabourette or Flower Stand. Made of solid oak and highly polished. Height, 18 inches; size of top, 13x15 inches. Very artistic, and makes a fine jardiniere stand. Weight, 15 lbs. A bargain.
Price, only.........................$1.35

No. 320 Tabourette. A little larger and finer finished than No. 302. Height, 22 in.; top, 15x15 in. Made of the most select quarter-sawed oak, and highly polished. By placing a pretty palm on one of these tabourettes you will find it to be very furnishing and exceedingly artistic. Weight, 20 lbs.
Price, only $2.45

$25-$45

No. 328 Tabourette. Made of solid mahogany and highly polished. Top and sides are all richly inlaid. Height, 21 in.; top, 14x14 in. There is nothing prettier for your parlor. Weight, 20 lbs

Price, only.........................$6.30

No. 327 Tabourette. This beautiful flower stand is made of quartered oak or solid mahogany, highly polished. Height, 22 inches; size of top, 22x22 inches. A little beauty and price very low. Weight, 20 lbs.
Price, quartered oak...............$3.15
Price, solid mahogany 3.85

No. 324 Tabourette. Is highly hand polished and made of solid mahogany, Top and sides are all beautifully inlaid with fancy wood. Height, 20 in.; top, 14x14 in. Artistic and a refined piece for the parlor.

Price, only $4.25

$25-$45

Parlor Tables and Jardiniere Stands

No. 105 Parlor Stand. This table will more than please you. Made of quarter-sawed oak or mahogany finish, richly hand carved and highly polished. Size of top, 18x33 inches. Satisfaction guaranteed. Very ornamental. Weight, 30 pounds.
Price, only $3.75

$75-$90

No. 179 Parlor Table. This is a little beauty for the money, and can't help but please. Made of the finest quarter-sawed oak and highly hand polished. Size of top, 24x24 inches. Has lower shelf and pretty French legs. Highly finished and price low.
Price, only $3.85

$40-$50

No. 195. This beautiful new design is made of quartered oak or solid mahogany, and beautifully hand polished. Has a 26-x26 fancy shaped top with French legs and pretty supports. Weight, 50 lbs.
Price, quartered oak, $3.30   Price, solid mahogany, $7.10

$45-$65

No. 176 Parlor Stand. Very artistic and pretty. Made of select quarter-sawed oak. Has French legs, well braced. Size of top, 20x20 inches. The stock used in this table is beautiful and will guarantee satisfaction. Weight, about 30 pounds.
Price, only $2.80

$35-$50

Parlor Tables and Jardiniere Stands

No. 142. Another new design in a pretty Tea or Parlor Table. Size of top, 16x28 inches. Has ornamental lower shelves for odd cups and saucers. Made of select bird's eye maple and mahogany finish; is beautifully hand polished and a very artistic and ornamental design. Weight, 15 pounds. A bargain. Price, only $5.10

$65-$80

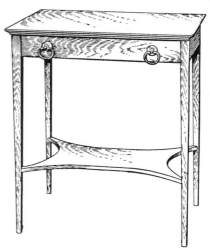

No. 189 Parlor, Bedroom or Sitting Room Table. Made of select bird's eye maple or solid mahogany, and is beautifully hand polished. Size of top, 16x24 in. Has one drawer and ornamented with brass and pearl handles. Owing to the extreme plain design the grain shows beautifully. Nothing finer made. Weight, 40 lbs. Price, only....................$3.95

$35-$55

No. 187 Parlor Table. Very plain and artistic design. Made of quarter-sawed oak, hand carved and polished like a piano. The stock in this table is beautiful and select. Size of top, 20x26 inches. A beauty for little money. Price, only $4.80

$45-$60

No. 173 Parlor Table. Extra good value. Made of quarter-sawed oak and polished. Size of top, 26x26 inches. Has a large shaped top and lower shelf, with fancy supports. Exceedingly ornamental. Just the thing for a large parlor and sitting room. Good size for a lamp and books. Weight, 50 pounds. Our bargain price is only........................$4.90

$45-$60

Parlor Tables and Jardiniere Stands

No. 131 Parlor Table. Made of solid mahogany or quartered oak. Has a round 24-inch fancy top, with French legs and rim under the top is inlaid. Beautifully polished. Weight, 40 pounds.
Quartered oak.................................$6.30
Solid mahogany............ ....7.70

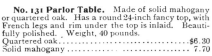

$45-$65

No. 124 Parlor or Library Table. Made of quartered oak or solid mahogany. Has large shaped top, 20x28 inches, and artistic French legs. The stock in this table is beautiful and can't help but please. Has shaped ends and sides. High grade in every respect. Weight, 45 pounds.
Price, in quartered oak $6.10
Price, in solid mahogany......................7.25

$30-$55

No. 193 Parlor Table. Made of quartered oak or solid mahogany. Highly hand polished. Has a large 22x28 shaped top, with graceful French legs, well braced. Good size and design. Weight, 45 lbs.
Price, in quartered oak.........................$4.55
Price, in solid mahogany........................5.25

$30-$55

No. 105 Parlor Stand. Made of quartersawed oak and highly hand polished. Top, 18x18 inches. Has lower shelf and French legs. Finish extra fine, and stock the best. Weight, 35 pounds.
Price, only $2.15

$30-$50

Ladies' Dressing Tables

No. 253 Ladies' Dressing Table. Made of quartered oak, bird's eye maple, curly birch or solid mahogany. Beautifully polished, sides and front of drawer richly inlaid. Has one drawer with pearl and brass handles, also a pretty 14x22-inch oval French bevel mirror. Size of top, 16x32 inches. Price, quartered oak...........................$14.00
Price, bird's eye maple, curly birch or solid mahogany............. 17.50

$75-$110

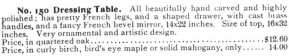

No. 150 Dressing Table. All beautifully hand carved and highly polished; has pretty French legs, and a shaped drawer, with cast brass handles, and a fancy French bevel mirror, 14x22 inches. Size of top, 16x32 inches. Very ornamental and artistic design.
Price, in quartered oak..$12.60
Price, in curly birch, bird's eye maple or solid mahogany, only...... 14.00

$75-$115

No. 251 Dressing Table. A little beauty. Made in all woods and beautifully hand polished. Size of top, 16x32 inches. Has a fancy 14x22-inch French bevel mirror, one drawer with pearl and brass handles, and all beautifully inlaid. Will more than please you if you want something extra fine. Weight, 50 pounds. Price, in quartered oak......$15.00
Price, in curly birch, bird's eye maple or solid mahogany........... 18.75

$75-$115

Parlor Tables

No. 160. This beautiful round table is made of mahogany or quartered oak; has a 28-inch top, with inlaid lines on mahogany. This makes a very artistic piece for the center of a room. Weight, 45 pounds.
Price, quartered oak...$6.95
Price, solid mahogany... 9.25

$50-$75

No. 168 Parlor or Library Table. Size of top, 22x35 inches. Has one drawer, with pearl and brass pulls, and a large lower shelf, with twisted pillars. Weight, 65 pounds. Price, quartered oak..........$7.75
Price, solid mahogany... 9.80

No. 134 Fancy Parlor Table. Has a fancy top and French legs; highly hand polished. Size of top, 20x30 inches. The stock is beautiful and the design is plain but artistic. Weight, 40 pounds.
Price, in quartered oak...$6.30
Price, in solid mahogany..... .... 7.70

$50-$70 $45-$70

Parlor Tables

No. 156 Parlor Table. Colonial design and exceedingly artistic; has large twisted legs, and a 26-inch round top and a heavy base. Made of select quartered oak or solid mahogany. Worth double our price. Weight, about 50 pounds. Price, in quartered oak..........................$ 7.70
Price, in solid mahogany... 10.50

$60-$80

No. 176 Parlor Table. This is one of the best designs in our line. Made of select quartered oak; hand carved and highly polished. Size of top, 26x26 inches. Has a shaped top and a large lower shelf, with a fancy railing and French legs; very ornamental, well made and large. Good size for a lamp and books. Weight, 50 pounds. Price, only......$5.95

$75-$100

No. 190 Parlor or Library Table. Made of the most select solid mahogany; has a large shaped top, 25x25 inches; has French legs, with a large shelf and carved mahogany supports; is beautifully hand polished. Nothing handsomer made. Weight, 60 pounds.
Price, in solid mahogany...$8.75

$50-$75

Parlor Tables

No. 137 Parlor or Library Table. This beautiful colonial design is made of oak or solid mahogany; has a large 26x26-inch oval top, supported by heavy rope design legs, resting on brass feet and a heavy base. This is handsome enough for any home. Weight, 65 pounds.
Price, in quartered oak..$ 9.10
Price, in solid mahogany..11.90

$60-$80

No. 146 Parlor or Library Table. Made of select quartered oak; beautifully hand polished. Size of top, 24x36 inches. Has a large lower shelf, one drawer and cast brass handles. Good size and well made. Weight, 77 pounds. Price, in quartered oak only..... ....$6.95

$45-$60

No. 138 Parlor or Library Table. Has a large 32x32-inch fancy shaped top and French legs, with fancy supports. The stock in this table is beautiful and made with swell ends and sides. There is nothing finer in design and construction. Price, in quartered oak..................$11.95
Price, in solid mahogany...14.70

$60-$80

Parlor Desks

No. 59 Parlor Desk. This is a beauty and a design that will more than please you. Made in all woods. Width, 27 inches. Inside partitioned with pigeon holes and drawer; has a brass railing on top and pretty French legs. Very artistic and a rich design.

Price, quartered oak...$5.60
Price, solid mahogany.. 6.95
Price, bird's-eye maple.. 5.60

$90-$120

No. 60 Parlor Desk. A handsome and artistic design. Made in all fancy woods. Has French legs, and the drop leaf is beautifully hand carved. Inside is partitioned with pigeon holes and drawer. Also one large drawer, fitted with fine cast brass handles, and a brass railing on top. Nothing made finished finer than this piece. Width, 27 inches; weight, about 59 pounds.

Price, quartered oak or bird's-eye maple $7.70
Price, solid mahogany 9.75

$90-$120

No. 62 Parlor Desk. Made of the finest and most select stock, and beautifully hand carved. Has French legs and cast brass handles. Inside is partitioned with pigeon holes and drawer. Has one large drawer, and is a very ornamental design. Width, 30 inches; weight, 60 pounds.

Price, in quartered oak..$ 9.10
Price, in bird's-eye maple.. 9.15
Price, in solid mahogany 11.20

$110-$130

Parlor Desks

No. 3 Fancy Desk. Good design and large size. Made of quarter-sawed oak or mahogany finish, carved and polished. Height, 51 inches; width, 30 inches. Inside partitioned with pigeon holes and drawer. Has a large drawer under drop leaf and French legs. A beauty for the money and a bargain. Weight, 75 pounds.
Price, only...............................$6.95

$115-$130

No. 2 Fancy Parlor Desk. Made of quarter-sawed oak or mahogany finish, and also in bird's-eye maple, and highly polished. Height, 49 inches, width, 27 inches. Inside is nicely partitioned with pigeon holes and drawer; also has a large drawer under drop leaf. Weight, 50 pounds. Good value.
Price, only.....................................$5.60

$115-$130

No. 1 Fancy Parlor Desk. Well-made, of solid oak or mahogany finish, carved and highly polished. Height, 40 inches; width, 24 inches. Inside is nicely partitioned with pigeon holes and small drawer; also, large drawer under drop leaf. Very ornamental and cheap. Weight, about 40 pounds. A bargain at our price.
Price, only...................................$4.25

$100-$115

No. 5½ Parlor Desk. Made of quartered oak or solid mahogany. Width, 27 inches. Inside is nicely partitioned with pigeon holes and drawer. Has French legs and large drawer. Beautifully hand carved, and polished like a piano. Weight, 60 pounds.
Price, quartered oak...........................$7.70
Price, bird's-eye maple.........................8.40
Price, solid mahogany..........................9.25

$125-$135

Parlor Desks

No. 4 Fancy Desk. Very odd and showy design. Height, 52 inches; width, 27 inches. Has a pretty 6x26-inch French bevel mirror, two small drawers, a large shelf and French legs. Inside is nicely partitioned with pigeon holes and drawer. Weight, 75 pounds.

Price, in bird's-eye maple or solid mahogany....................................$11.20

$150-$175

No. 67. This beautiful little French Leg Desk is made in all woods. Beautifully polished and carved. Has one drawer made with shaped front and cast brass handles. Inside partitioned with pigeon holes and drawer. Width, 28 inches.

Price, quartered oak..............................$13.30
Price, bird's-eye maple...........................14.65
Price, solid mahogany............................16.65

$100-$115

No. 65 Parlor or Fancy Desk. Made of select stock, hand polished and carved. Width, 26 inches. Has one drawer and pretty French legs. Inside partitioned with pigeon holes and drawer. Weight, 60 pounds.

Price, in quartered oak.......................$ 9.70
Price, in bird's-eye maple.....................10.75
Price, in solid mahogany......................12.00

$100-$115

No. 61 Parlor Desk. A graceful and artistic design. Made of select stock. Width, 30 inches. Inside is nicely partitioned with pigeon holes and drawer. Has pretty French legs and two drawers under drop leaf. Weight, 60 pounds.

Price, in quartered oak..........................$11.25
Price, in solid mahogany.........................14.00

$125-$145

Book Cases

No. 461 Bookcase. Well made of quartered oak or mahogany finish and highly hand polished. Height, 5 feet; width, 2 feet 1 inch. Shelves are adjustable. Our price on this case is very low. Has a large glass door, and a great deal of room, as it has 5 shelves. Weight, 95 lbs.
Price, only..........................$6.75

$130-$160

No. 462 Bookcase. Made of quartered oak or mahogany finish, hand carved and highly polished. Exceedingly ornamental and useful. The design is very artistic and rich. Height, 5 feet 4 inches; width, 2 feet 6 inches. All shelves are adjustable, and the glass in door is extra good quality. Has the open lattice work in top of door, which is very pretty. Weight, 95 lbs. Price..........................$8.45

$150-$200

No. 463 Bookcase. Extra good value. Well made of quartered oak, carved and highly polished. Height, 6 feet 1 inch; width, 2 feet 10 inches. Has 1 drawer in lower part and open lattice work in top of door. All shelves are adjustable. Good size and style. Will guarantee satisfaction on all our bookcases. Weight, 125 lbs.
Price..........................$13.85

$200-$250

No. 465 Bookcase. Made of quartered oak, carved and highly hand polished. Height, 6 feet; width, 2 feet 7 inches. Has 2 fine French bevel mirrors 6x12, and a glass door. Also has a glass cabinet with door in top, and a large shelf. All shelves are adjustable. Weight, 125 lbs. A bargain.
Price, only..........................$14.85

$200-$250

Book Cases

No. 396 Bookcase. Made of the finest quarter-sawed oak, hand carved and polished. Height, 6 feet 2 inches; width, 4 feet 1 inch. Has a large 8x38 inch French bevel mirror. This is a very heavy, well made case, and also has large polished pillars on sides. Shelves are adjustable, and fine glass in doors. Weight, 120 lbs. Price....................$16.70

$225-$275

No. 464 Bookcase. This is a perfect beauty for the money. Very artistic and ornamental. Made of quartered oak or mahogany finish, richly carved and polished. Height, 5 feet 8 inches; width, 3 feet. Has a good 8x30 inch French bevel mirror. All shelves are adjustable. Weight, 125 lbs. Price. $14.40

$225-$275

No. 466 Bookcase. Very large and well made. Made of quartered oak, carved and polished. Height, 6 feet; width, 3 feet 5 inches. Has a pretty 10x16 French bevel mirror, a small shelf on top and open lattice work in top of door, which is very ornamental. All shelves are adjustable. Very roomy, well made and cheap. Weight, 125 lbs. Price............ $15.90

$325-$375

Book Cases

No. 469 Bookcase. Made of the best quarter-sawed oak, hand carved and highly polished. Height, 6 feet 3 inches; width, 3 feet 9 inches. The glass in doors is of a fine quality, and shelves are adjustable. Also a small drawer in lower part, and open lattice work in upper part of door. Weight, 150 lbs. Price...$18.05

$300-$350

No. 467 Bookcase. Very large and a rich design. Made of quarter-sawed oak, hand carved and highly polished. Height, 5 feet 9 inches; width, 3 feet 9 inches. Has a very fine French bevel mirror 6x42 inches. All shelves are adjustable and doors are fitted with the best quality of glass. Weight, 150 lbs. Price....................................$18.90

$225-$275

No. 468 Bookcase. Made of the best quarter-sawed oak, hand carved and highly polished. Height, 5 feet 11 inches; width, 3 feet 10 inches. Has a good 12x20 inch French bevel mirror. The glass in doors is of a fine quality, and shelves are adjustable. Also a small drawer in lower part and open lattice work in top of door. Weight, 180 lbs. Price..$21.50

$325-$375

Combination Desk and Library Cases

No. 473 Combination Bookcase and Writing Desk. Made of quarter-sawed oak, hand carved and highly polished. Height, 6 feet 4 inches; width, 4 feet. Has a French bevel mirror 16x22 inches. The two drawers under desk are shaped, and the glass door is ornamented with open lattice work. All shelves are adjustable. Inside of desk is partitioned. Well made and cheap. Weight about 150 pounds.
Price, only $23.40

$325-$375

No. 471 Combination Bookcase and Writing Desk. Made of solid oak or mahogany finish, hand carved and highly polished. Height, 6 feet; width, 4 feet 1 inch. Shelves are adjustable. Desk has drop leaf, which is beautifully carved, and inside is nicely partitioned with pigeon holes and drawers. Has a good French bevel mirror, 16x20 and one 8x18 inches. Weight about 150 pounds. Good value, well made and cheap. Has three large drawers, made with shaped fronts and swell shaped glass in the door.
Price, only $26.95

$275-$300

Large Library Cases

No. 140 Bookcase. Made of the finest quartered oak, hand carved and polished. Height, 6 feet 10 inches; width, 5 feet 2 inches. Has brass rods and rings for curtains, and all shelves are adjustable. Large and well made. Weight, 95 pounds.
Price, only...$12.85

$225-$300

No. 118 Bookcase. This is by far the most artistic and refined style in our stock. Quarter-sawed oak, hand carved and highly hand polished. Made with a heavy base, and a heavy rope molding at top. All shelves are adjustable, and extra fine glass in the doors. Height, 60 in.; width, 36 in.; two doors. Weight, about 100 pounds.
Price, only...$12.60
No. 119. Same, only larger, 4 feet 2 inches wide, and two doors............................. 14.75
No. 120. Same, only larger, 5 feet 3 inches wide, and three doors............................ 17.95

$225-$300

Large Library Cases

No. 154 Bookcase. Very large and massive design. Made of quarter-sawed oak, hand carved and highly polished. Height, 5 feet; width, 6 feet. All shelves are adjustable and doors are fitted with the best quality of glass. Has heavy molding all around the top. Weight, 130 pounds.
Price $23.95
No. 153. Same, only 5 feet wide 20.25
No. 152. Same, only 4 feet 2 inches, and two doors 16.75

$275-$325

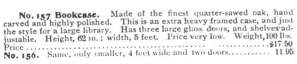

No. 157 Bookcase. Made of the finest quarter-sawed oak, hand carved and highly polished. This is an extra heavy framed case, and just the style for a large library. Has three large glass doors, and shelves adjustable. Height, 62 in.; width, 5 feet. Price very low. Weight, 100 lbs.
Price $17.50
No. 156. Same, only smaller, 4 feet wide and two doors 11.95

No. 470 Bookcase. Quarter-sawed oak, richly hand carved and polished like a mirror. Height, 6 feet 3 inches; width, 5 feet 3 inches. Has three large glass doors and a small drawer for magazines, and open lattice work in top of center door. All drawers are adjustable. If you want a large, heavy, well made case, this will please you.
Price $24.55

$250-$300

$475-$575

Combination Book Cases

No. 444 Combination Bookcase. Here is a combination case that will give satisfaction, and is by far the best case on the market for the money. Oak or mahogany finish, carved and polished. Shelves are adjustable. Height, 5 feet 10 inches; width, 3 feet 3 inches. French bevel mirror, 12x14 inches. Desk is partitioned with pigeon holes and drawer, also a large door under desk for magazines. Weight, 120 pounds. A bargain Price, only...$9.95

$200-$225

No. 477 Combination Bookcase and Writing Desk. Made of quarter-sawed oak or mahogany finish, and highly polished. Height, 5 feet 9 inches; width, 3 feet 8 inches. Has a good fancy French bevel mirror, 14x16 inches. Shelves are adjustable. Inside is partitioned. Has 2 small shelves above bookcase for bric-a-brac, and a drawer and cupboard below desk. Weight, about 140 pounds.
Price...$12.95

No. 404 Combination Bookcase and Writing Desk. Made of quarter-sawed oak or mahogany finish, hand carved and highly polished. Height, 5 feet 9 inches; width, 3 feet 7 inches. Has a fancy 12x16 inch French bevel mirror. All shelves are adjustable. Desk is partitioned with pigeon holes and drawers, and has 1 drawer and cupboard below desk. Weight, about 150 pounds. Good value.
Price, only...$14.80

$200-$225

$250-$300

101

Combination Book Cases

No. 475 Combination Bookcase and Writing Desk. Made of quarter-sawed oak or mahogany finish, hand carved and highly polished. Height, 6 feet 1 inch; width, 3 feet 9 inches. Has a French bevel mirror, 14x20 inches. All shelves are adjustable. Inside of desk is partitioned. Has 3 large drawers fitted with cast brass handles and locks. Well made and cheap. The shelves above desk are artistic and ornamental. Weight, about 150 pounds.
Price...$18.75

$300-$375

No. 443 Combination Bookcase and Writing Desk. Made of quarter-sawed oak or mahogany finish, hand carved and highly polished. Height, 6 feet; width, 3 feet 9 inches. Has a good French bevel mirror, 16x16 inches, also has the pretty open lattice work in top of door. All shelves are adjustable. Inside is partitioned. Has one large drawer and door under desk fitted with locks and cast brass handles. Weight, 140 pounds. A bargain.
Price, only...$16.75

$270-$325

No. 432 Combination Bookcase and Writing Desk. Made of solid oak or mahogany finish, hand carved and highly polished. Height, 6 feet; width, 3 feet 8 inches. Shelves are adjustable. Desk has drop leaf. Inside is nicely partitioned with pigeon holes and drawers. Has a good French bevel mirror, 16x18 inches. Weight, about 150 pounds. Good value, well made and cheap. Has 2 large drawers and a cupboard with locks. Price, only...$17.60

$250-$300

Combination Book Cases

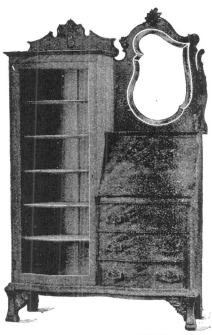

No. 472 Combination Bookcase and Writing Desk. Made of the finest quartered oak or mahogany finish, neatly carved and highly polished. Height, 6 feet 2 inches; width, 3 feet 10 inches. Has 3 large drawers made with swell front, and a large 16x24 French bevel mirror. All shelves in bookcase are adjustable, and the glass in the door is shaped. Desk is nicely partitioned with pigeon holes and drawer. Weight, 200 pounds. Price...$23.95

$215-$250

No. 442 Combination Bookcase and Writing Desk Combined. Quartered oak, beautifully hand carved and polished. Height, 6 feet 2 inches; width, 3 feet 9 inches. Has a large French bevel mirror, 17x23 inches. Has 3 large drawers with swell front and cast brass handles. All shelves are adjustable.
Price..$19.95

$250-$300

No. 441 Combination Bookcase and Writing Desk. Quartered oak, hand carved and highly polished. Height, 6 feet; width, 4 feet 1 inch. Has a beautiful 16x22 French bevel mirror, and 3 swell front drawers with cast brass handles under desk. All shelves are adjustable. A beauty and nothing handsomer made. Weight, 200 pounds.
Price..$24.95

$230-$270

China Cabinets

No. 452 Corner China Cabinet. Quartered oak and polished. The stock in all our cabinets is of the finest grain; you surely will be pleased with them. This is a plain, but rich design. Height, 5 feet 5 inches; width, 2 feet 7 inches. Made with swell front and shaped glass in the door. We will submit other designs of corner cabinets if desired. Weight, 120 lbs. Price, only.........................$11.95

$325-$375

No. 451 China Cabinet. Select quartered oak and beautifully polished. Height, 5 feet 10 inches; width, 2 feet 5 inches. Has a fancy French bevel mirror in top, size 10 x 24 inches. Glass in the door and sides is of the best quality. The door is ornamented with lattice work; rich, new and pretty. Weight, 110 lbs. Price.......................$13.30

$230-$275

No. 450 China Cabinet. Made of select quartered oak and beautifully polished. Height, 5 feet 5 inches; width, 2 feet 5 inches. Has a large glass door and glass sides, and all shelves are adjustable. Good size and at a very low figure. Weight, 100 lbs. Price, only............................$9.95

$175-$225

No. 366 China Cabinet. Made of quartered oak, hand carved and highly polished.- Height, 5 feet 4 inches; width, 2 feet 6 inches. The glass in door and sides is of the best quality. Has a pretty 6 x 20 inch French bevel mirror in top. An artistic design, and an ornament to any dining-room. Weight, 100 lbs. Price, only..$11.30

$200-$225

China Cabinets

No. 454 China Cabinet. Quartered oak, hand carved and highly polished. Height, 5 feet 11 inches; width, 2 feet 7 inches. Made with serpentine front and shaped glass in the doors, and glass ends. Has a large, fancy 8 x 26 inch French bevel mirror in top. Is a very artistic and handsome design; worth double our price. Weight, 140 lbs. Price...........$18.65

$300-$375

No. 457 China Cabinet. Quartered oak, hand carved and highly polished. Height, 5 feet 8 inches; width, 3 feet 1 inch. The best quality of glass in the door and sides. Has a large glass cabinet on top with glass door, which contains a large 12 x 30 inch French bevel mirror. Very ornamental and graceful design. Weight, 190 lbs. Price......................$19.95

$550-$600

No. 449 China Cabinet. A very artistic and rich design; one of the best patterns on the market. Made of quartered oak, hand carved and beautifully polished. Height, 5 feet 5 inches; width, 2 feet 5 inches. Has five large shelves and the best glass in door and sides. Weight, 110 lbs. Price......$16.60

$250-$325

No. 455 China Cabinet. Large and roomy. Selected quartered oak, hand carved and highly polished. Height, 5 feet 8 inches; width, 3 feet 4 inches. Has a 6x18 inch fancy French bevel mirror, and swell shaped glass in the sides. Weight, 160 lbs. Price $17.95

$375-$450

China Cabinets

No. 346 China Cabinet. A large, rich and massive design. Made of the finest quartered oak, hand carved and nicely polished. Height, 6 feet; width, 4 feet 6 inches. Has large, carved claw feet, and swell shaped glass in the ends. The glass is of the finest quality and the stock is beautiful. Weight, 240 lbs. Price...........................$29.25

$475-$525

No. 456 China Cabinet. Made of select quartered oak, hand carved and beautifully polished. Height, 6 feet 2 inches; width, 4 feet 1 inch. Has a large, fancy 8x36 inch French bevel mirror, and swell shaped glass in the ends. French legs, and contains a great deal of hand carving. Weight, 210 lbs; worth $40.00. Our price.......................$22.60

$450-$525

No. 459 China Cabinet. Contains the finest of quartered oak and is beautifully hand polished. Height, 5 feet 8 inches; width, 3 feet 10 inches. The door is made with swell front and shaped glass. The front is ornamented with open lattice work—something entirely new—and is very artistic. Has five large shelves, and best quality of glass in the ends. Weight, 240 lbs. Price,.......................$26.60

$425-$475

Sideboards

No. 435 Sideboard. Made of quartered oak, richly carved and polished. Size of top, 24x48 inches. Has a large 18x32 inch German bevel mirror. Height, 6 feet 2 inches. One drawer is lined with velvet for silverware. A good sensible design and one that will please you in every way. Satisfaction guaranteed. Price............................$13.70

$225-$250

No. 410 Sideboard. Made of quartered oak, carved and polished. Size of top, 24x48 inches. Has a good, large 18x32 inch German bevel mirror. One drawer lined with velvet for silverware. All drawers have locks and handles made of cast brass. All the drawers work smoothly and the cabinet work is of the best. Weight, 200 pounds. Price, only ..$16.00

$250-$275

No. 415 Sideboard. A beauty for the money. A good, heavy design. Richly hand carved and highly polished. Made of quartered oak. One drawer lined with velvet for silverware, and handles made of cast brass. Size of top, 26x48 inches. Has a large 18x40 German bevel mirror. Weight, 200 pounds. Price, only................................$17.50

$200-$225

Sideboards

No. 470 Sideboard. Very large and heavy design. Size of top, 25x48 inches. Made of the finest quarter-sawed oak, hand carved and highly polished. Has an extra large 18x40 oval French bevel mirror. Handles made of cast brass, the lower doors and top drawers are made with swell front. One drawer lined with velvet for silverware. Price, only..$25.50

$375-$400

No. 441 Sideboard. A good, heavy, massive design. Richly hand carved and highly polished. Made of quartered oak. One drawer lined with velvet for silverware, and handles made of cast brass. Middle drawer made with swell front and the base is all beautifully hand carved. Size of top, 25x48 inches. Has a fine 18x40 German bevel mirror. Price, only..$20.75

$325-$375

No. 406 Sideboard. Made of quarter-sawed oak, carved and polished. Size of top, 25x48 inches. A large 18x36 inch French bevel mirror. Height, 6 feet 4 inches. One drawer lined with velvet for silverware. A rich and handsome design. The middle top drawer is made with swell front and the base is all beautifully carved. Weight, 200 pounds. This will more than please you. Price, only..$23.60

$375-$400

Sideboards

No. 76½ Sideboard. Very large and massive. Made of the finest quarter-sawed oak, hand carved and highly polished. Size of top, 24x58 inches. Has a very large 20x48 inch French bevel plate mirror. Middle top drawer is made with swell front, and has cast brass handles. One drawer lined for silverware. Weight, 300 pounds. Price.........$42 80

$300-$350

No. 490 Sideboard. Here is a style that is hard to beat. Very large and handsome. Made of select quarter-sawed oak, hand carved and highly polished. Size of top, 25x48 inches. Has a large 20x40 inch French bevel mirror. Lower doors are made with swell front, and handles made of cast brass and has rope moulding facing. Drawer lined for silverware. Price, only.....................................$27.95

$275-$300

No. 320 Sideboard. A rich sideboard for little money. Worth double our price. Made of fine quarter-sawed oak, hand carved and highly hand polished. Has a fine large 20x38 inch French bevel mirror. Size of top, 25x54 inches. Has swell front and sides, and handles are made of the finest cast brass. One drawer lined for silverware. A handsome and artistic design. It contains the best cabinet work and highest polish. Price.....................................$33.85

$325-$375

Sideboards

No. 641 Sideboard. Has a large 18x40 inch French bevel mirror, two small drawers, one of them partitioned and lined for silverware, one long drawer for linen, and two doors in base. Made of quartered oak, in antique or Flemish finish. This is the best and cheapest sideboard on the market in Flemish finish.
Price....................................$27.75

$225-$275

No. 638 Sideboard. Quartered oak, in antique or Flemish finish. 4 feet 6 inches wide, 5 feet 1 inch high, with 16x44 inch French bevel mirror. One long drawer, three small drawers and double closet in base, and center drawer lined for silver.
Price, only............................$36.50

$200-$250

No. 639 Sideboard. Quartered oak, finished antique or Flemish. Height, 5 feet 11 inches; width, 4 feet 6 inches, with one 14x46 and one 10x46 inch French bevel mirrors in top. Has 3 small drawers and double closet in base and center, small drawer lined for silverware.
Price.................................$40.50

$300-$325

Sideboards

No. 643 Sideboard. A handsome and artistic design. Quartered oak in antique or Flemish finish; 4 feet wide and 6 feet high, with one 14x40 inch French bevel mirror under shelf and a closet over shelf with one 12x40 inch mirror in back and clear glass in front and ends. Has a sensible base; large and roomy.
Price $39.20

$325-$375

No. 640 Sideboard. Quartered oak in antique or Flemish finish. Height, 6 feet; width, 4 feet 6 inches, with a 14x46 inch French bevel mirror under shelf and a closet over shelf with a 12x46 mirror in back and clear glass in front and ends. Has three small drawers and double closet in base and one drawer lined for silverware.
Price. $36.00

$325-$375

No. 642 Sideboard. Quartered oak in antique or Flemish finish. Height, 5 feet 8 inches; width, 4 feet, with one 8x40 and one 14x40 inch French bevel mirrors. Two small and one large drawers and double cupboard in base.
Price, only. $33.60

$275-$300

China Closets

No. 1542 Corner China Closet. Quartered oak, antique or Flemish finish. 35 inches wide in front and 65 inches high. Has spiral fluted and twisted pillars. A very effective design, making a refined frame for chinaware. Price, only $23.80

$375-$450

No. 1541 China Closet. This beautiful closet has the spiral fluted and twisted pillars, French legs and shaped glass in ends. Height, 5 feet 6 inches; width, 3 feet 6 inches. Quartered oak, antique or Flemish finish. Refined and artistic design. Price. $28.60

$375-$450

Table and Chairs

No. 232 Dining-Room Table.
Quartered oak, antique or Flemish finish. Size of top, 48 inches. The heavy twisted legs and carved mouldings give a very stylish effect. Length, when open, 10 feet.

Price.....................$25.25

$175-$200

These Dining-Room Chairs are made of quartered oak, finished antique or Flemish. Match the other goods on this page. Has twisted posts and neat carving on the rails.

No. 80 Diner. Cane seat, each...............$4.25
Leather seat, each.... 4.85

No. 80½ Arm Chair, to match cane seat, each.$7.45
Leather seat 8.15

No. 68 Diner. Leather spring seat, each...........$7.80

No. 68½ Arm Chair. To match No. 68; leather seat, each.............$11.70

NO. 80 CHAIR

$40-$50

NO. 68 CHAIR

$60-$65

Combination Sideboards, China Closets

No. 450 Sideboard and China Closet Combined. Made of the finest quartered oak, hand carved and highly polished. Has a large 14x48 French bevel mirror, and a china closet with glass door and sides; size, 14x21x52 inches; height from base, 16 inches. Back is covered with silk plush. Size of top, 26x54 inches. Small middle drawers are shaped and one is lined with velvet for silverware. A very handsome, refined and artistic design. Height, 6 feet 6 inches. Weight, 275 lbs. Price, only..$47.95

$300-$350

No. 426 Sideboard. With china cabinet in the top. Made of the most select quartered oak, hand carved and polished. Has a 12x44 French bevel mirror, and a china closet with glass above base, size 14x16x48; size of top, 25x48 inches. The 4 top drawers are made with swell front, and 1 drawer is lined with velvet for silverware. Height, 5 feet 10 inches. All drawers have locks and cast brass handles. Weight, 200 lbs. Price..$31.95

$225-$275

No. 475 Sideboard. Quartered oak, hand carved and polished. Has one 10x44 and two 6x24 French bevel mirrors. Has a china cabinet in top, size 11x15x38, and stand 12 inches from base. Base is richly shaped and made with swell front. Size of top, 25x48 inches. Has a glass shelf, mirror back, and glass doors in the top cabinet. Height, 6 feet 6 inches. Very artistic and elegant design. Weight, 200 lbs. Price, only....$42.60

$350-$425

Combination Sideboards, China Closets

No. 414 Sideboard and China Closet Combined. Made of quartered oak, hand carved and highly hand polished. Height, 6 feet 1 inch; width, 4 feet 9 inches. Has a large china closet at the left with glass door and ends, and shelves are adjustable. The entire front is shaped and swell glass in the door. Has a large 24x28 French bevel mirror, 2 pretty shelves and French legs. Very ornamental and artistic design. Weight, 200 lbs. Price, only...$43.90

$350-$400

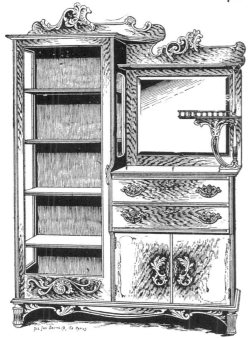

No. 416 Sideboard and China Closet Combined. Made of quarter-sawed oak, hand carved and highly polished. Height, 77 inches; width, 51 inches. Has large 20x22 French bevel mirror. The closet at the left has a large glass door with best glass in ends. All shelves are adjustable. Has brass cast handles. Weight, 200 lbs. Extra large and a bargain. Price...$28.20

$375-$425

No. 412 Sideboard and China Closet Combined. Made of quartered oak, hand carved and highly polished. Height, 6 ft.; width, 4 ft. 5 inches. Made with swell front and has a large 22x24 French bevel mirror. The cabinet at the left has a large glass door and glass ends and all shelves are adjustable. Has cast brass handles, beautifully polished. One drawer lined with velvet for silverware. Weight, 200 lbs. Price, only.....$33.25

$350-$400

Music Cabinets

No. 10 Music Cabinet. A very desirable style. Your music is always clean in this, as it has a door and lock. Made of select quartered oak or mahogany finish, neatly carved and highly polished. Height, 42 inches; width, 20 inches. Weight, 60 lbs. Price..$5.95

No. 10½. Same as No. 10, except is made without the door, and has a brass rod with rings for curtain. Price only $4.75

$75-$100

No. 11 Music Cabinet. Made of quarter-sawed oak, richly hand carved and highly polished. Very ornamental and a handsome design. Inside is nicely arranged with shelves. Has a large door and a drawer at top with locks. Height, 45 inches; width, 20 inches. Weight, 60 lbs. Price, only $6.95

$90-$110

No. 12½ Music Cabinet. Made of quartered oak or mahogany finish, richly hand carved and highly polished. Has a door and lock. Very ornamental and cheap. The inside is nicely arranged with shelves. Height, 43 inches; width, 20 inches. Weight, 60 lbs. Price $6.30

$75-$80

No. 12 Music Cabinet. Made of quarter-sawed oak or mahogany finish, richly hand carved and highly polished. Very ornamental and a handsome design. Has French legs and a pretty 5x14 inch French bevel mirror. Inside is nicely arranged with shelves. Has a large door with lock. Height, 47 inches; width, 20 inches. Weight, 65 lbs. Price, only $7.80

$75-$110

Extension Tables

No. 165 Extension Table. Extra large and heavy. Made of oak, richly carved **and** polished. Size of top, 44x44 inches. Legs are very large and well supported. A good **design,** and price is very low. Will last forever. Weight, 10-foot table, about 175 pounds.
Price, 8-ft. table.....$10.55   Price, 12-ft. table....$11.95   Price, 12-ft. table....$12.90

$115-$140

No. 162 Extension Table. Made of the finest quarter-sawed oak and highly hand polished. Top extra large; size, 44x44 inches. Has large turned legs, made of 6-inch stock. A rich design and made of beautiful stock. Slides guaranteed to work smoothly. Fitted with casters. Weight, 10-foot table, about 175 pounds.
Price, 6-ft. table...$8.45   Price, 8-ft. table...$9.70   Price, 10-ft. table..$10.90

$100-$115

Extension Tables

No. 166 Extension Table. This is an extremely artistic design. A table that is sure to please and rich enough for anyone. Made of the finest quartered oak, neatly carved and highly polished. Top is extra large and heavy. Size, 44x44 inches. Has extra large, heavy legs, well supported. The supports are richly hand carved. Weight about 175 pounds, Worth double our price.
Price, 8-ft. table..$14.45   Price, 10-ft. table..$15.65   Price, 12-ft. table..$16.85

$175-$200

No. 137 Extension Table. This is one of the best designs in our catalogue. A good, large, heavy table, and made to last forever. The stock is very select and beautiful. Made of select quarter-sawed oak, richly carved and polished like a piano. Size of top, 44x44 inches. Has extra heavy turned 6-inch legs, and well supported with heavy stock. Will guarantee satisfaction, and can be returned at our expense if not satisfactory. Weight, 175 pounds.
Price, 8-ft. table..$13.75   Price, 10-ft. table..$14.75   Price, 12-ft. table..$15.70

$150-$175

Extension Tables

No. 167 Extension Table. This table is made of the finest quarter-sawed oak, elaborately hand carved and polished like a mirror. Size of top, 48x48 inches. Nothing handsomer in the way of beautiful grained stock. Has large carved legs, and the supports are also richly hand carved. A massive and rich design. Weight, about 175 pounds.
Price, 8-ft. table.......$18.45   Price, 10-ft. table.....$19.65   Price, 12-ft.-table....$20.80

$200-$250

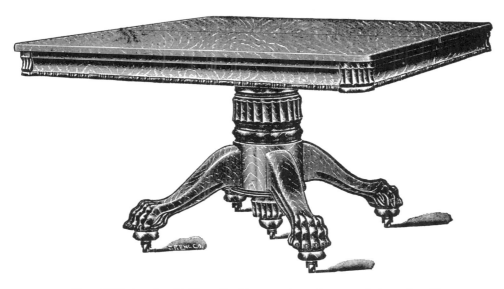

No 168 Extension Table. Nothing prettier and more artistic made. The lower part is all richly hand carved and has the large claw feet. The grain in the top is beautiful, and is polished like a piano. All made of the finest quarter-sawed oak. Size of top, 48x48 inches. If you want something elegant, buy this. Weight, 175 pounds.
Price, 8-ft. table..$19.00   Price, 10-ft. table..$20.00   Price, I2-ft. table..$21.25

$250-$300

Dining-Room Sets

No. 372 Dining-Room Set. A handsome design, artistic, correctly shaped and altogether a very taking pattern; stylish high back with brace arms. All points considered they are perfect. Made of quarter-sawed oak and nicely finished. Weight, 12 and 15 pounds.

Diners, in cane seat.....each, $ 1.55   Arm Chair...............$3.00
Diners, in cane seat...per doz , 18.00
One set: 5 Diners and 1 Arm Chair, cane seats, only $10.25
One set: 5 Diners and 1 Arm Chair, leather seats, only 14.00

$50-$60 $55-$75

No. 366CL Chair. A very attractive and a low-priced dining-room chair, with genuine leather seat, and back made of solid oak and nicely finished; medium high back. Weight, 13 pounds.

Price................each, $ 2.00
Price.............per doz., 23.00

No. 736 Dining-Room Set. This is a very showy, large shaped wood seat dining or sitting room chair; long posts, very strong and comfortable. Made of hardwood, and finished antique. The arm chair has bolted arms.

Diners............each, $ 1.10   Arm Chair......... each, $2.00
Diners.........per doz., 12.50
We will sell any number of above, but the proper way to buy them
    is in a set consisting of 5 Diners and 1 Arm Chair for only..$7.00

$40-$50 $45-$55 $50-$60

Dining-Room Sets

No. 726 Dining-Room Set. Polished quartered oak. Well made and beautifully finished. Has large seats, box framed and bolted. The back fits you to perfection.

Diner, cane seat...........each. $1.95	Per doz..............	$22.50
Diner, leather seat......... " 2 60	Per doz..............	30.00
Arm Chair, cane seat...... " 3.95		
Arm Chair, leather seat.... " 5.00		
Cane seat, 5 Diners and 1 Arm Chair.......................		$12.75
Leather seat, 5 Diners and 1 Arm Chair....................		17.00

$35-$40 $50-$60

No. 369 Dining-Room Set.
For description and price see No. 369A under this cut.

$40-$50

No. 716 Dining-Room Set. A special bargain. Full larger size, large seat, box framed and bolted; has fine shaped legs, spindle back. It needs no brace arms to make it strong. Made of white quartered oak and highly polished; cane or leather seats. Weight, 13 and 15 pounds.

Diner, cane seat ....each, $1.70	Per Doz..............	$19.50
Diner, leather seat......... " 2.40	Per Doz..............	27.00
Arm Chair, leather seat.... " 4.50		
Arm Chair, cane seat ...... " 3.50		
Cane seats, 5 Diners and 1 Arm Chair......................		$11.25
Leather seats, 5 Diners and 1 Arm Chair....................		15.00

$25-$35 $50-$60

Dining-Room Sets

No. 745 Dining-Room Set. This is one of the finest on the market. Handsome design; new and stylish. Made of the finest white oak, quarter-sawed and polished. Has large, shapely seat, easy to keep clean. Its equal never sold before for less than $40.00. The very best leather used on these goods.

Diner in leather.......each, $4.25   Diner in cane.........each, $ 2.95
Arm Chair in cane .... "   5 60   Arm Chair in leather. "   7.25
One set, five Diners and one Arm Chair, cane seats............. 20.00
One set, five Diners and one Arm Chair, leather seats........... 26.00
    Same in solid walnut for $3.00 a set extra.

$50-$75 $35-$50

No. 369A Dining-Room Set.
Medium high back. Made of quartered oak, nicely carved, large cane seat; backs are just high enough to be comfortable; also, a very ornamental chair, strong and showy; sure to please. Weight, 12 and 15 lbs.
Diner, cane seat... ...each, $ 1.75
Diner, cane seat....per doz., 20.00
Arm Chair....:...... .each, 2.95
One set : 5 Diners and 1 Arm
    Chair................... 11.00
One set : 5 Diners and 1 Arm
    Chair, in leather sets...... 15.35

$55-$65

No. 713 Dining-Room Set. This is a bolted box seat dining set. Full French legs, shaped seat, slat back; artistic and very attractive. Made of quartered white oak, highly polished. If you want the best, order this. It will serve you for 15 years or more. Weight of diner, 13 lbs.; arm chair, 18 lbs.
Cane seat Diner .... each, $ 2.30
Cane seat Diner ....per dozen, 26.00
Cane seat Arm Chair ....each, 4.25
One set, five Diners and one Arm Chair, only 15.00
One set five Diners and one Arm Chair, in leather seats, only 19.50

$25-$35 $40-$50

122

Dining-Room Sets

No. 747 Set. A handsome and artistic design. Bolted box seat, French legs, and nicely shaped seat. A practical dining-room set in every way; quartered oak and highly polished. Weight, 15 and 20 pounds.

Diner, cane seat, each............$3.25	Per dozen..................,......$36.00
Diner, leather seat, each..........3.95	Per dozen...................45.00
Arm Chair, cane seat............5.25	Arm Chair, leather seat.......6.25
Cane Set, 5 Diners and 1 Arm Chair.................................20.00
Leather Set, 5 Diners and 1 Arm Chair.................................24.50

$50-$55 $65-$75

No. 723 Set. Handsome design and very comfortable. Banister back, French legs, bolted box frame seats; quartered oak and polished. Will last a life time. Weight, 15 and 18 pounds.

FOR PRICE SEE CUT BELOW.

$30-$40

No. 727 Dining-Room Set. Artistic design, and a very shapely and comfortable back; easy to keep clean. Has a bolted box framed seat, quartered oak and highly polished. Will last a life time.

Diner, cane seat, each.... ....$3.00	Per dozen.................... ....$34.50
Diner, leather seat, each..........3.70	Per dozen...................42.50
Arm Chair, cane seat, each.......5.50	Arm Chair, leather seat, each. 6.50
Cane Set, 5 Diners, 1 Arm Chair.................................19.00
Leather Set, 5 Diners, 1 Arm Chair.................................25.00

$30-$40 $50-$75

Dining-Room Sets

No. 783 Set. Another very fine leather seat and back dining-room set. Large spring seats and best leather; finest material throughout, very shapely and artistic. Made of the finest quartered oak and polished. If you want the best, you will be pleased with this. Weight 15 and 20 pounds.

Diner, each	$ 7.50
Per dozen	87.00
Arm Chair	10.00
One Set, 5 Diners and 1 Arm Chair	45.00

$50-$75 $75-$100

Arm Chair to No. 723 Dining-Room Set.

No. 723 Diner, cane seat, each	$ 2.30
Per dozen	26.00
Diner, leather seat, each	2.95
Per dozen	34.00
Arm Chair, cane seat, each	4.25
Arm Chair, leather seat, each	5.25
Cane Set, 5 Diners and 1 Arm Chair	14.50
Leather Set, 5 Diners and 1 Arm Chair	19.00

$70-$80

No. 758C Set. Our Flemish Dining-Room Set. Very artistic; tapestry or leather seat. These twist or rope carvings are all the rage now; very large and massive, strong, durable and comfortable. Antique oak, polished, Flemish, oak or mahogany finish. Weight, 15 and 20 pounds.

Diner, each	$ 6.50
Per dozen	75.00
Arm Chair	9.50
One Set, 5 Diners and 1 Arm Chair, only	40.00

$75-$100 $75-$100

Old Hickory Chairs for the Lawn or Porch

No. 42 Large Arm Chair. Good size and extra heavy stock. Well made and very comfortable. Back is extra high. Weight, 18 pounds. Price, only....................$3.75

No. 43 Rocker, to match above. Price, only....................$4.25

$45-$55

No. 53 Large Arm Rocker. All nicely shaped. Has high back and is extremely comfortable. Very artistic and ornamental. Weight, 15 pounds. Price..............,.....$4.55

No. 44 Chair, to match above Price, only....................$4.00

$50-$75

No. 32 Lawn or Porch Chair. Hickory. Well made, and will last for years. A bargain at our price. Only.......................$1.95

No. 33. Rocker to match above. Weight, 10 pounds. Only.....$2.35

$50-$60

No. 35 Porch Rocker. Made of hickory. Back is extra high and very comfortable. Nothing more artistic made than this line. Weight, 11 lbs. Price, only $2.70

No. 34. Chair to match above. Only.................. ......$2.40

$50-$75

No. 106 Old Hickory Settee. Has shape back and sides, which makes it very comfortable. Length, 40 inches. Weight, 25 pounds. Will last for years in any climate. Price, only...$5.05

No. 107. Same as above on runners, making a very comfortable rocker settee. Price, only $5.50

$50-$80

Office Desks

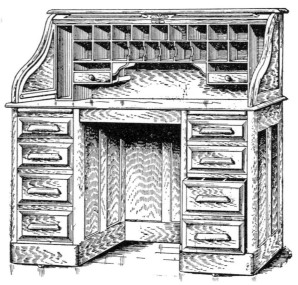

No. 229 High Curtain Office Desk. Height, 49 inches; length, 4 feet; width, 30 inches. Solid oak and hand polished. Has lap joint, dust and knife proof curtain. Solid oak writing bed, painted on the back to prevent warping. Two sliding arm rests. Automatic drawer lock, which is operated by curtain. All drawers are 12 inches wide inside, and two drawers are partitioned in each pedestal. Satisfaction guaranteed or money refunded. Extra good value. Weight, 245 pounds. Price, only...$19.50
No. 228. Same as No. 229, except is 4 feet 6 inches long. Price 19.75

$450-$500

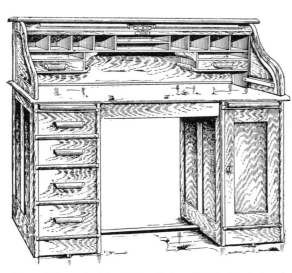

No. 246 Low Curtain Office Desk. This is the best and cheapest desk of its size on the market. Well made of solid oak, and polished. Has lap joint, dust and knife proof curtain. Length, 4 feet; width, 32 inches; height, 45 inches. A solid oak writing bed. Painted on the back to prevent warping. Two sliding arm rests. Automatic drawer lock, which is operated by curtain. All drawers are 10½ inches wide inside. Book racks in pedestal are 17 inches high and 11½ inches deep. Pigeon holes are 3x4 inches. Weight, 200 pounds. Price, only...........$12.65

$300-$375

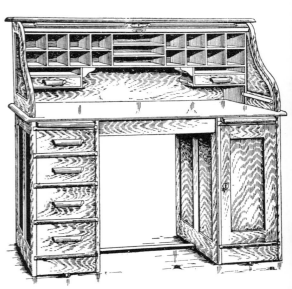

No. 245 High Curtain Office Desk. Well made of solid oak and highly polished. Is a good size and a bargain at our price. Height, 49 inches; length, 4 feet 2 inches; width, 32 inches. Has lap joint, dust and knife proof curtain. A solid oak writing bed. Two sliding arm rests. Automatic drawer lock, which is operated by curtain. All drawers are 10 inches wide inside. Book racks in pedestal are 17 inches high. Satisfaction guaranteed or money refunded. Weight, 210 pounds. Price, only...$14.50

$340-$390

Office Desks

No. 225 Extra High Curtain Office Desk. Made of entirely quarter sawed oak. Has a heavy double top and carved handles. Highly hand polished. Pigeon holes are conveniently arranged. The right side has a door with lock; also has a large drawer in center with Yale lock. Length, 5 feet; height, 50 inches; width, 34 inches. Has raised panels all around and full molding base. A solid oak writing bed. Two sliding arm rests. An automatic lock, operated by curtain. Drawers are 12 inches wide inside. Two drawers partitioned in each pedestal. Pigeon holes, 3x4 inches. Weight, 315 pounds. Price..............................$34.45
No. 224. Same as No. 225, except is 5 feet 6 inches long. Extra large size. Weight, 235 pounds. Price..........................$38.85

$500-$575

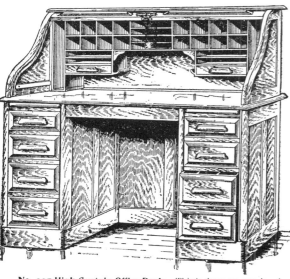

No. 227 High Curtain Office Desk. This is the most popular size and the best seller in our line. Made of select oak and highly polished. Length, 5 feet; width, 32 inches; height, 49 inches. Has a solid oak writing bed, guaranteed not to warp. Two sliding arm rests. Automatic drawer lock, operated by the curtain. Drawers are 12 inches wide inside. Pigeon holes are 3x4 inches. Two drawers in each pedestal are partitioned. Has full moldings around the base. Weight, 280 pounds. Worth double our price. Only....................................$20.50

$450-$500

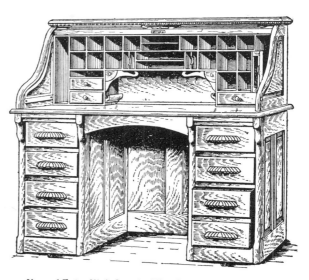

No. 226 Extra High Curtain Office Desk. Made of quarter-sawed oak, hand polished. Has our special built-up writing bed. Has lap joint, dust and knife proof curtain. All drawers are partitioned and finished inside. Has full moldings around base of each pedestal, and dust and mouse proof bottoms. Two sliding arm rests. Automatic lock, which is operated by curtain. Weight, 300 pounds. Height, 50 inches; length, 4 feet 6 inches; width, 34 inches. Price..................................$29.90

$500-$575

Office Desks

No. 239 Flat Top Office Desk. Made of oak and polished. Length, 4 feet; width, 32 inches. Oak bed, painted on back to prevent warping. Finished back. Drawers are 12 inches wide inside. Two drawers are partitioned and has sliding arm rests. One machine lock in top drawer locks all drawers automatically. Weight, about 175 pounds.
Price, only...$10.00
No 238. Same as No. 239, except is 4 feet 6 inches long. Price 11.60
No. 237. Same as No. 239, except is 5 feet long. Price....... 13.86

$100-$130

No. 236 Flat Top Office Desk. Extra fine. Made of quarter-sawed oak and highly hand polished. Has raised panels all around, and a drawer in center with Yale lock. Length, 4 feet 6 inches; width, 34 inches. Has our special built-up writing bed. Drawers lock automatically by the operation of the top drawer. Drawers are 12 inches wide inside, and fully partitioned. Two sliding arm rests. Weight, about 210 pounds.
Price...$18.75
No. 235. Same as No. 236, except is 5 feet long. Price....... 21.00

$100-$150

No. 240 Flat Top Office Desk. Made of select oak and highly hand polished. Length, 3 feet 6 inches; width, 2 feet 6 inches. Has a large drawer under writing bed and three large side drawers, and a sliding arm rest. A good size and a bargain at our price. Weight, 130 pounds.
Price, only...$9.50

$50-$100

TABLES - ROUND

$225-$250

$150-$165

$225-$250

$240-260

$235-$260

$350-$375

TABLES - ROUND

$150-$175

$160-$175

$200-$220

$240-$265

$165-$175

$240-$265

TABLES - ROUND

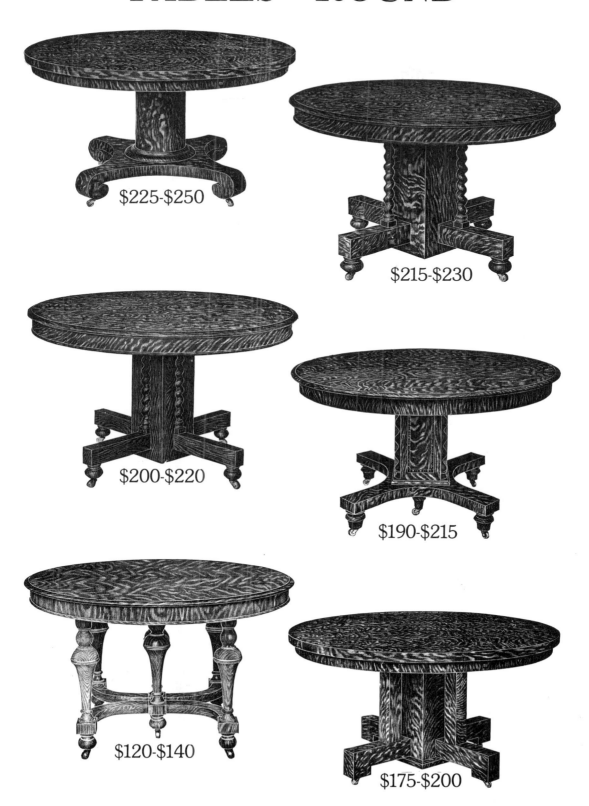

$225-$250

$215-$230

$200-$220

$190-$215

$120-$140

$175-$200

TABLES - ROUND

$130-$155

$215-$230

$240-$260

$160-$180

$230-$260

$220-$250

TABLES - ROUND

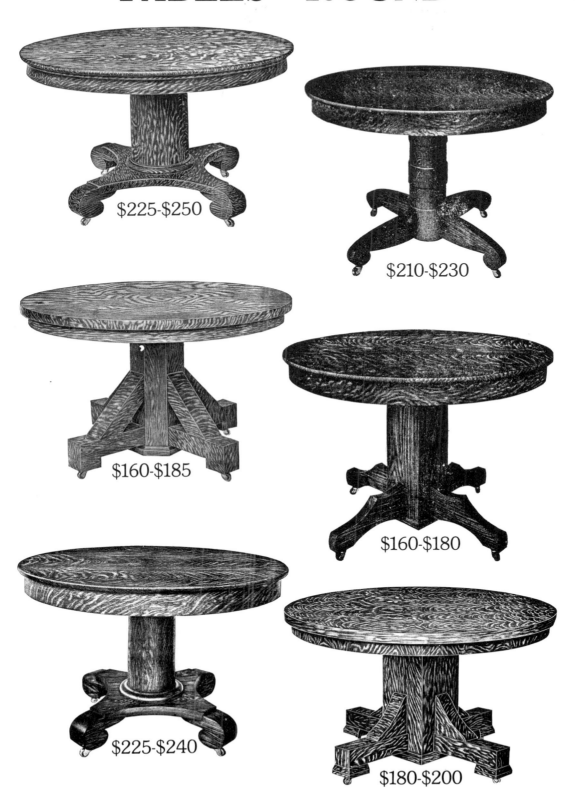

$225-$250

$210-$230

$160-$185

$160-$180

$225-$240

$180-$200